CODEX ABYSSUS

by

Volodymyr Bilyk

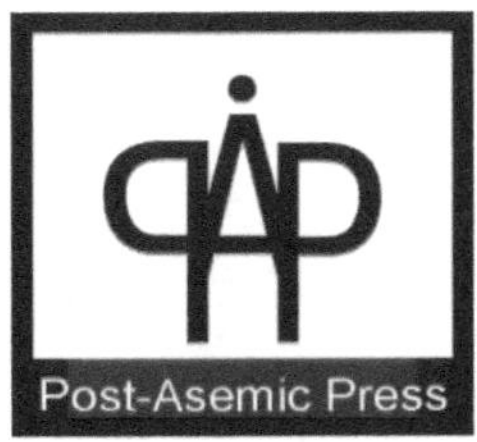

Post-Asemic Press 004

ISBN-13: 978-1-7328788-6-0

Contact: postasemicpress@gmail.com

Postasemicpress.blogspot.com

Codex Abyssus is in the lettrist vein, but the abysses I see (or imagine seeing), make it more conceptual, and coherent, and also funny. I look at an otherwise innocent circle or dot or a black rectangle, and see another pit, because the small icons (many of them definitely stairs, funnels, mazes, black rays from the underworld) interfere. The title is instructive of course, but this work could not be replaced with its description. The main reading pleasure comes from the fact that first I see, say, a window-like object, drawn with childlike simplicity, then I realize that it must open to a precipice, and I look down and start feeling dizzy. The great variety of compositions combines with a great economy of forms. After a while I already search for their abyss-like qualities. Expectations and impressions meet halfway. And each page, as a whole, too, has a third dimension, owing to the hand-drawn, irregular frames. Anything with contours becomes the icon of an abyss. Some icons are even multi-abyssed, for the sheer joy of creating danger, and escaping it (perhaps), in the same process. If you need ideas for falling, here are many-many options, tirelessly and playfully intuited.

Two-dimensional depth calling attention to itself is also a joke about representation. Thanks to this wise and humorous work, we are saved again and again by a new pit, precipice, abyss from the void of the blank page, from the fear of emptiness. But it is always momentary only. Who knows what comes next.

—Márton Koppány

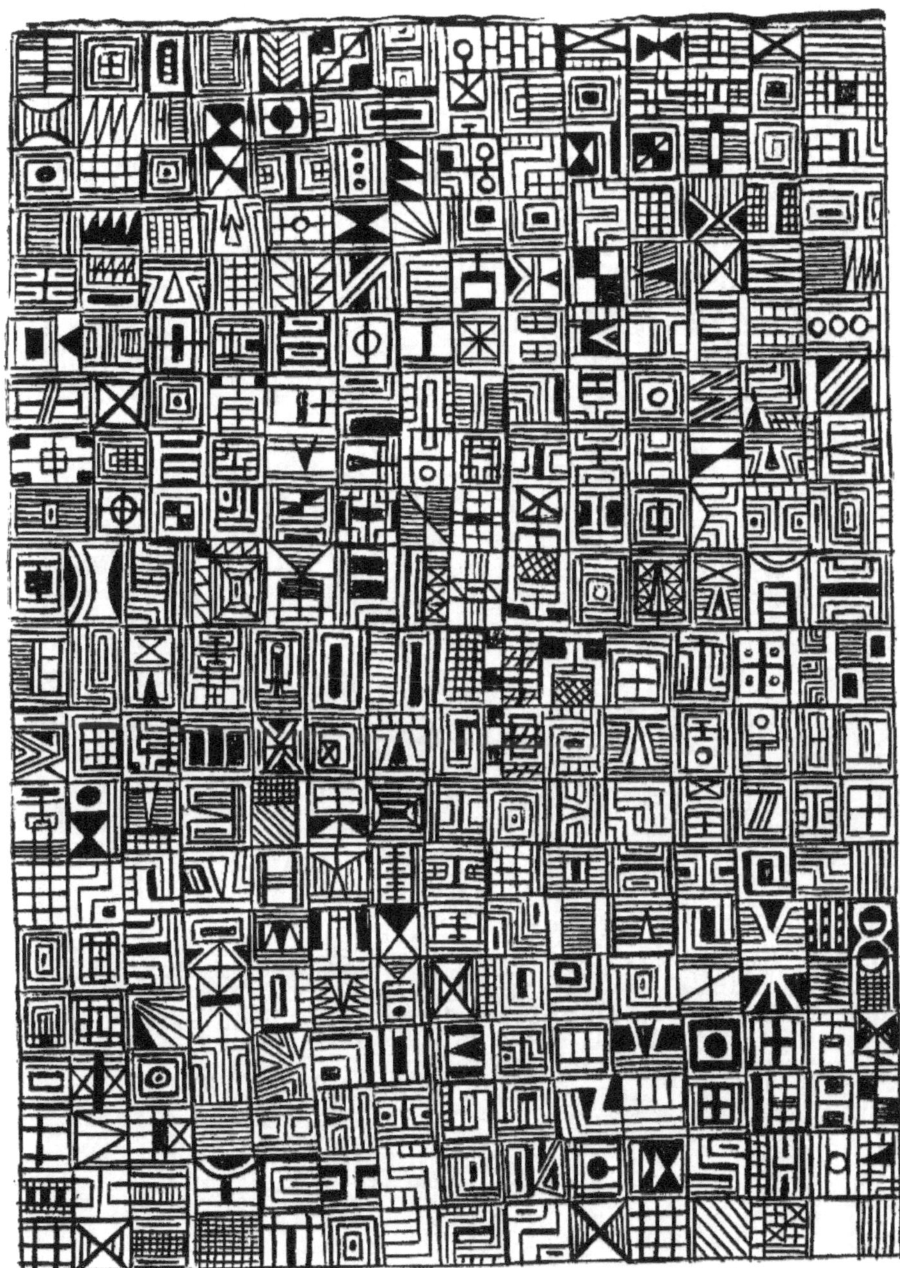

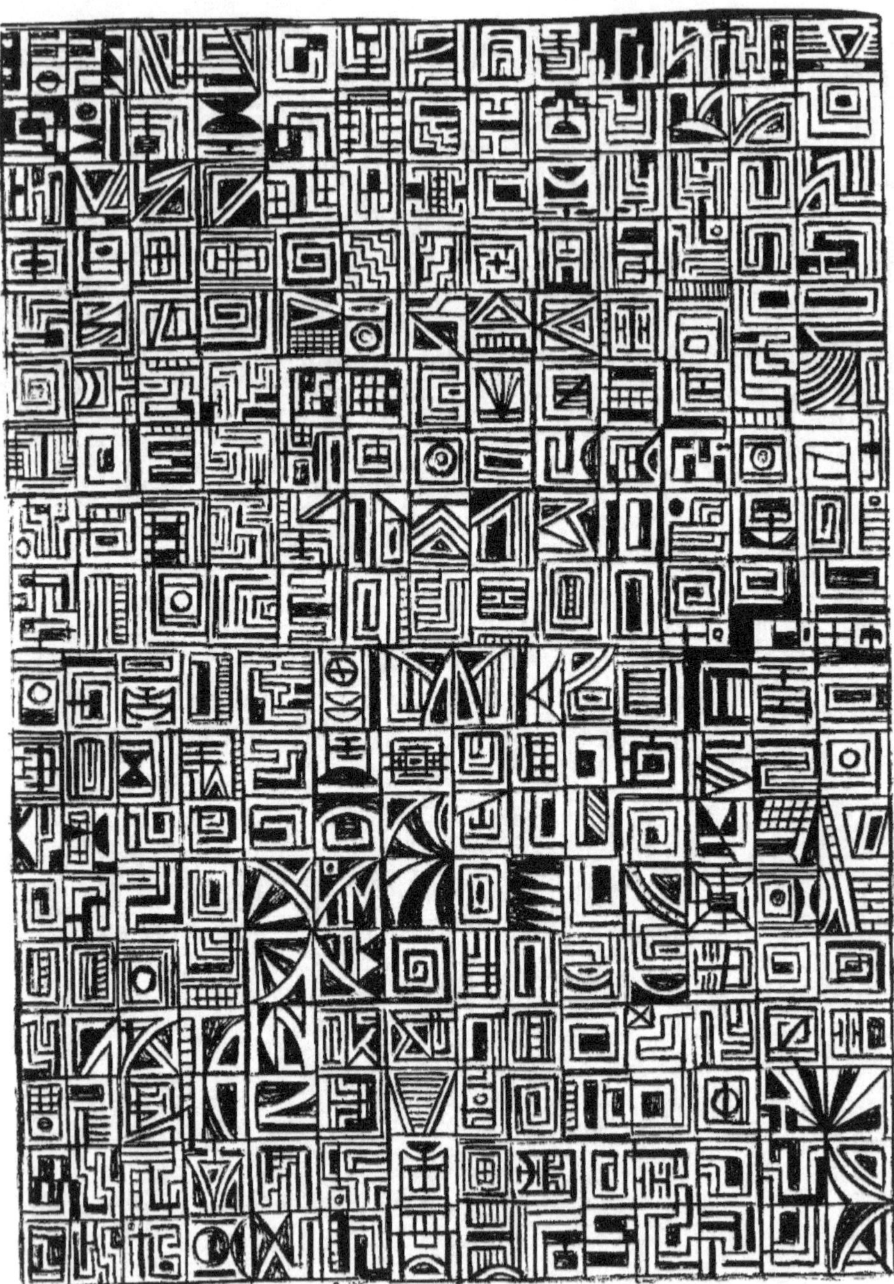

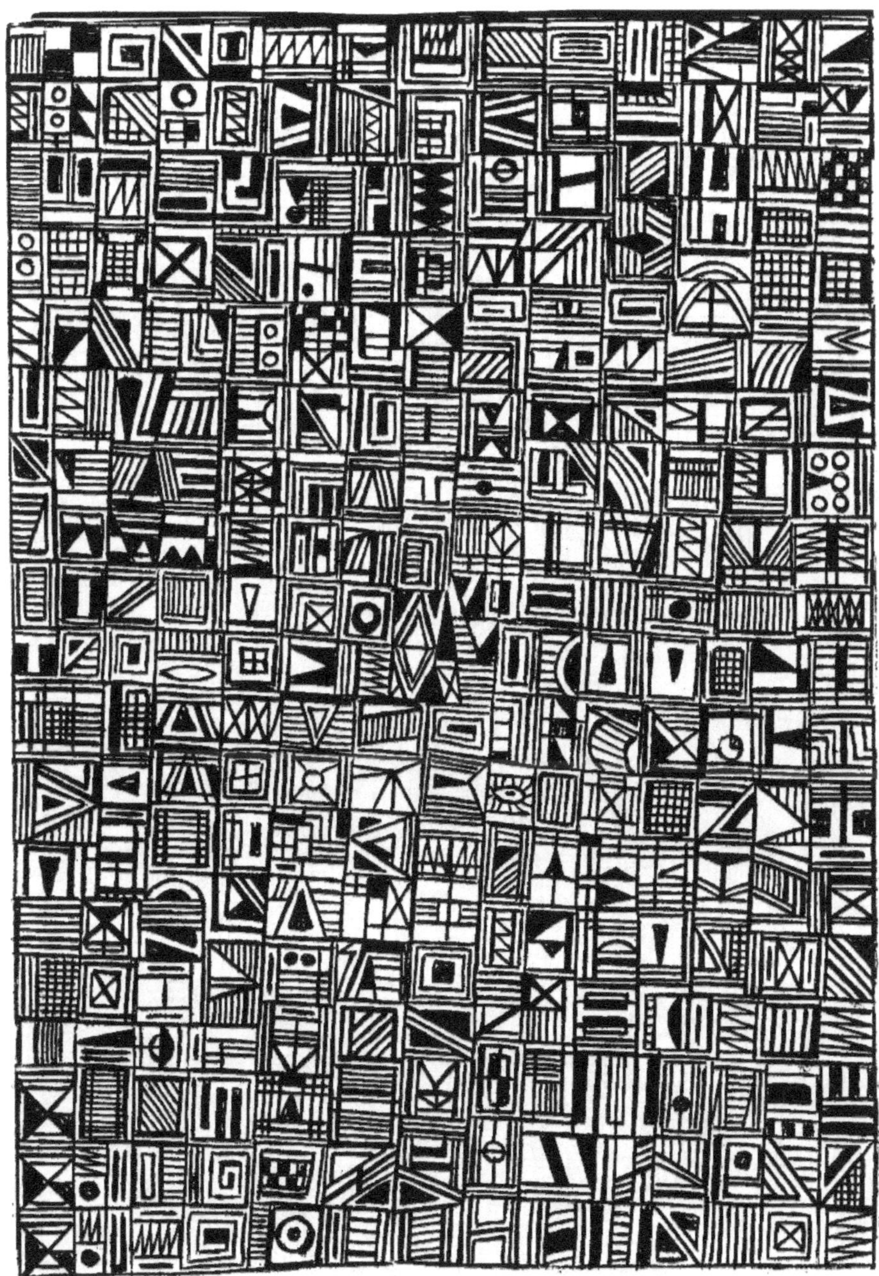

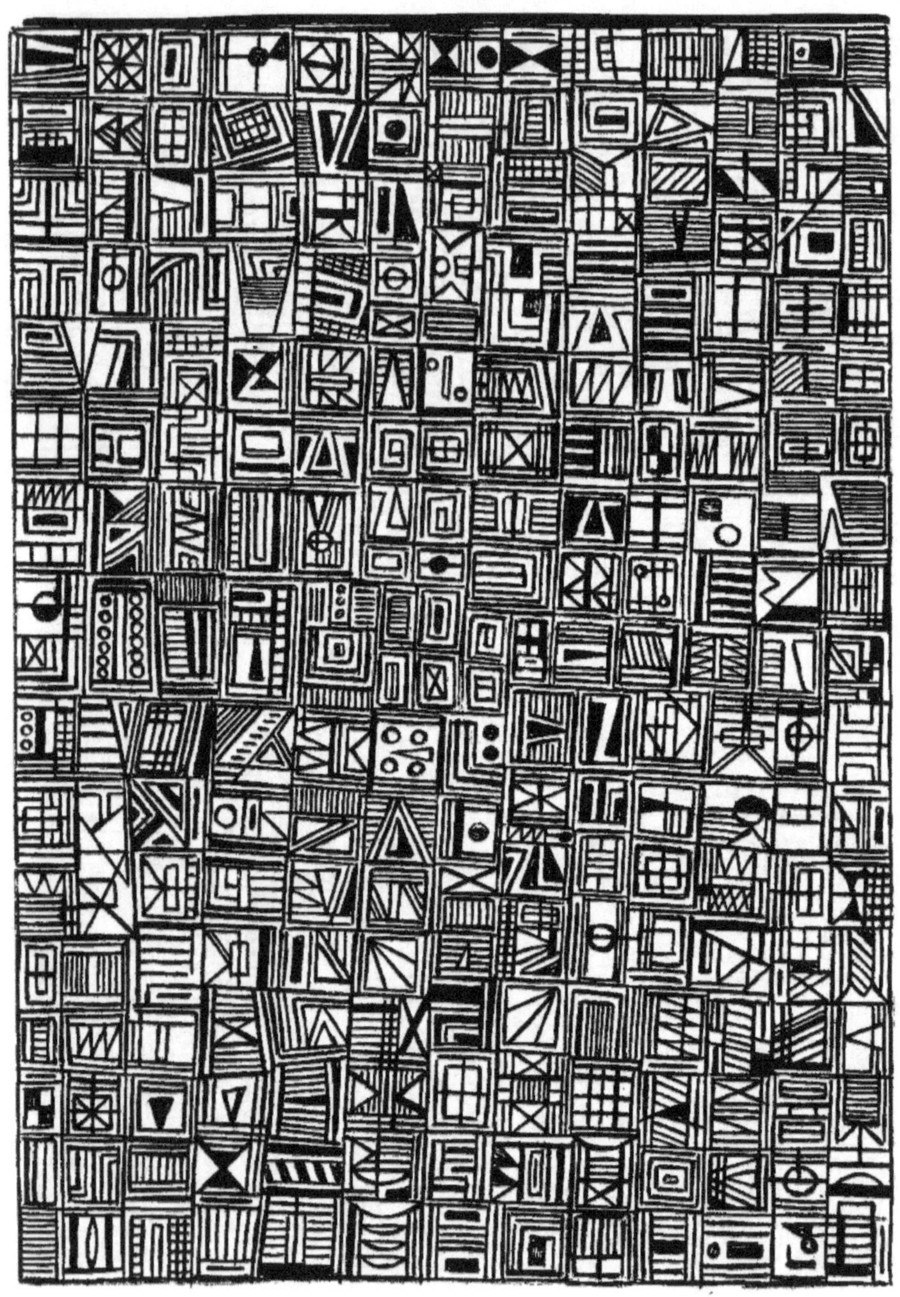

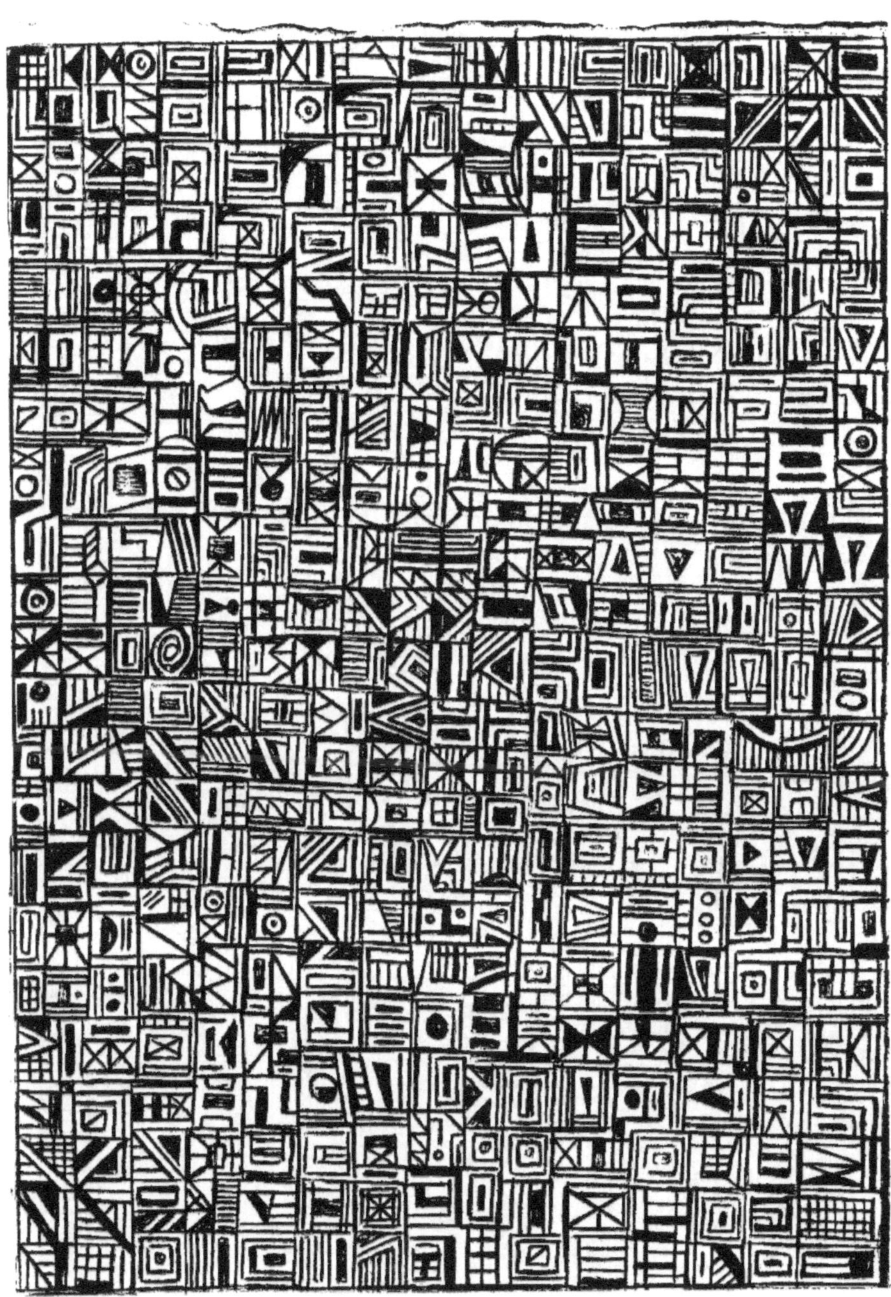

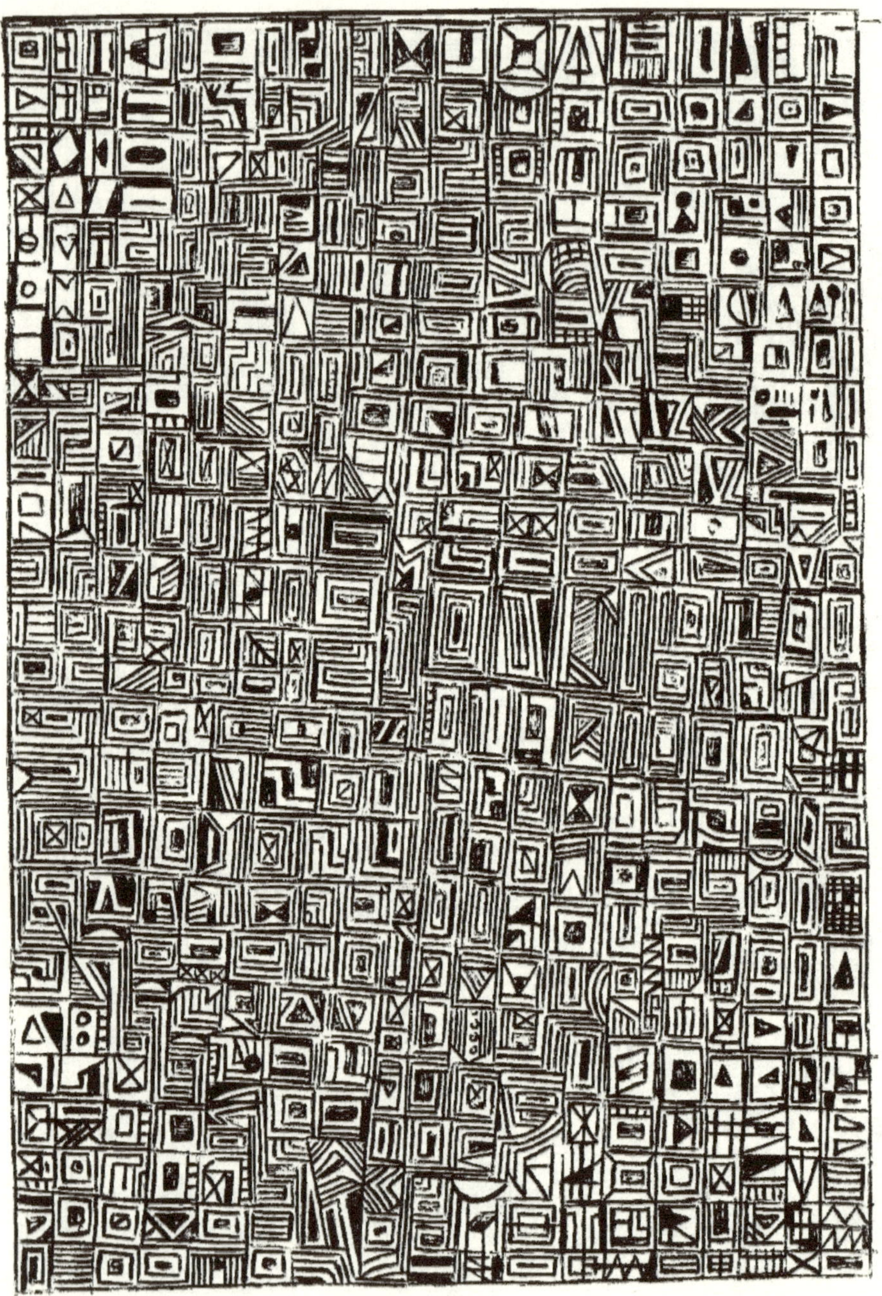

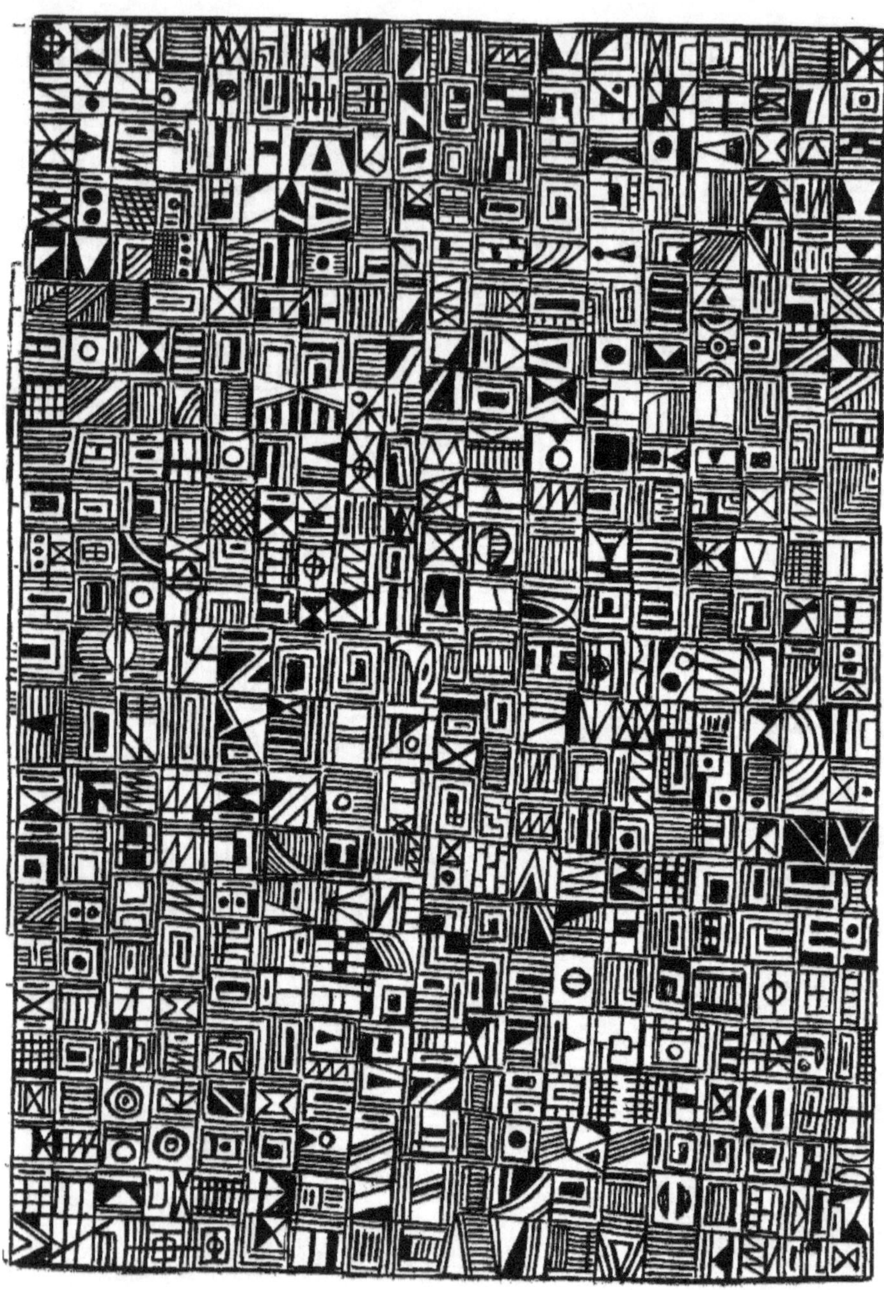

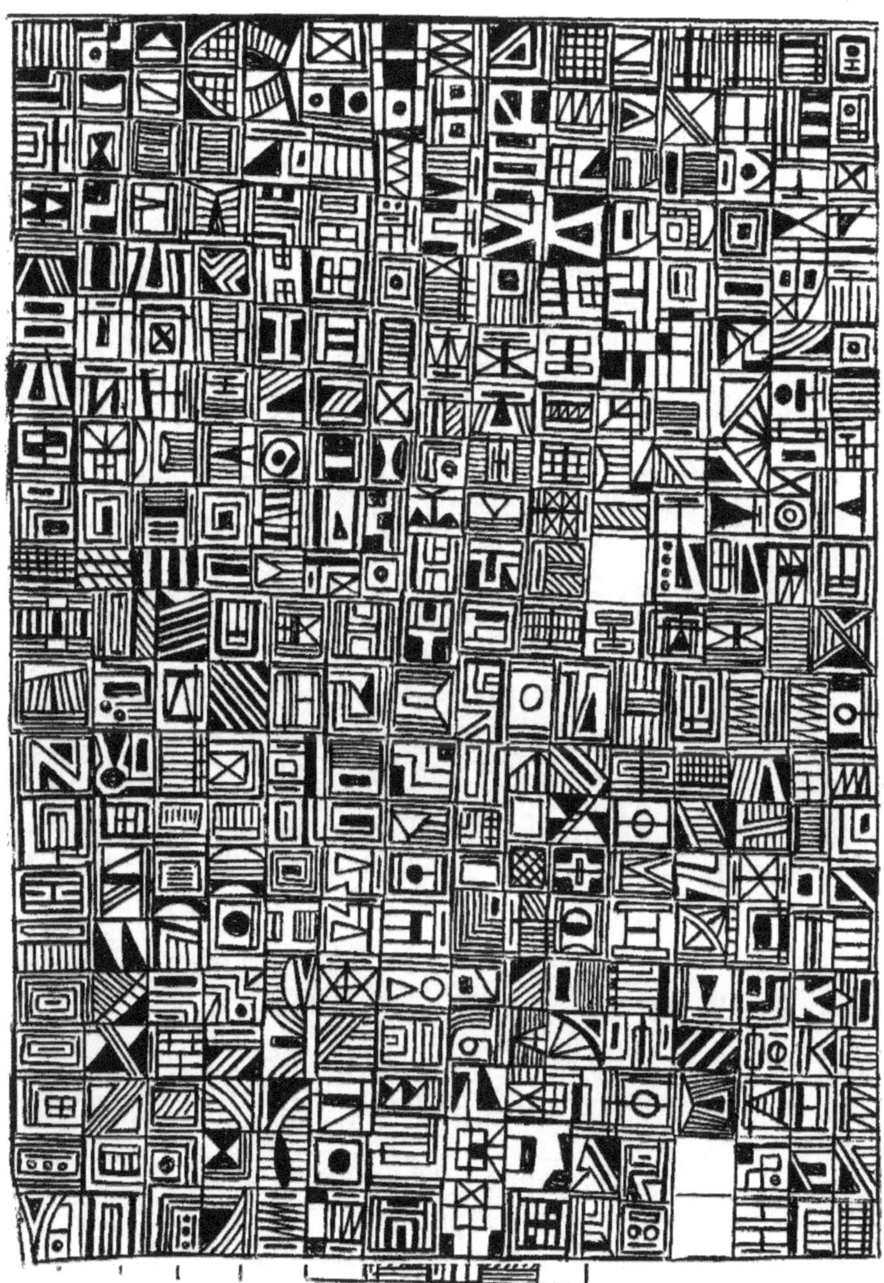

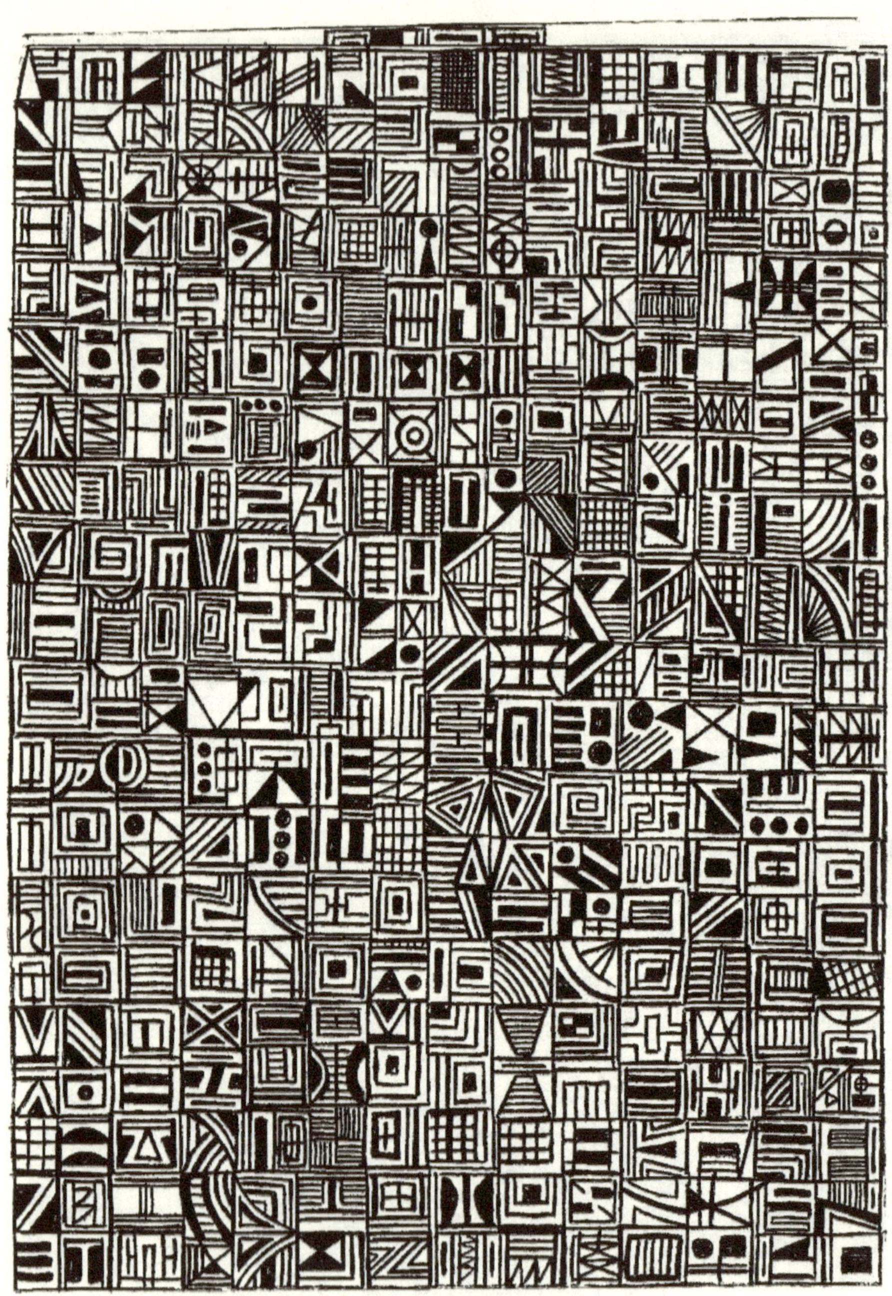

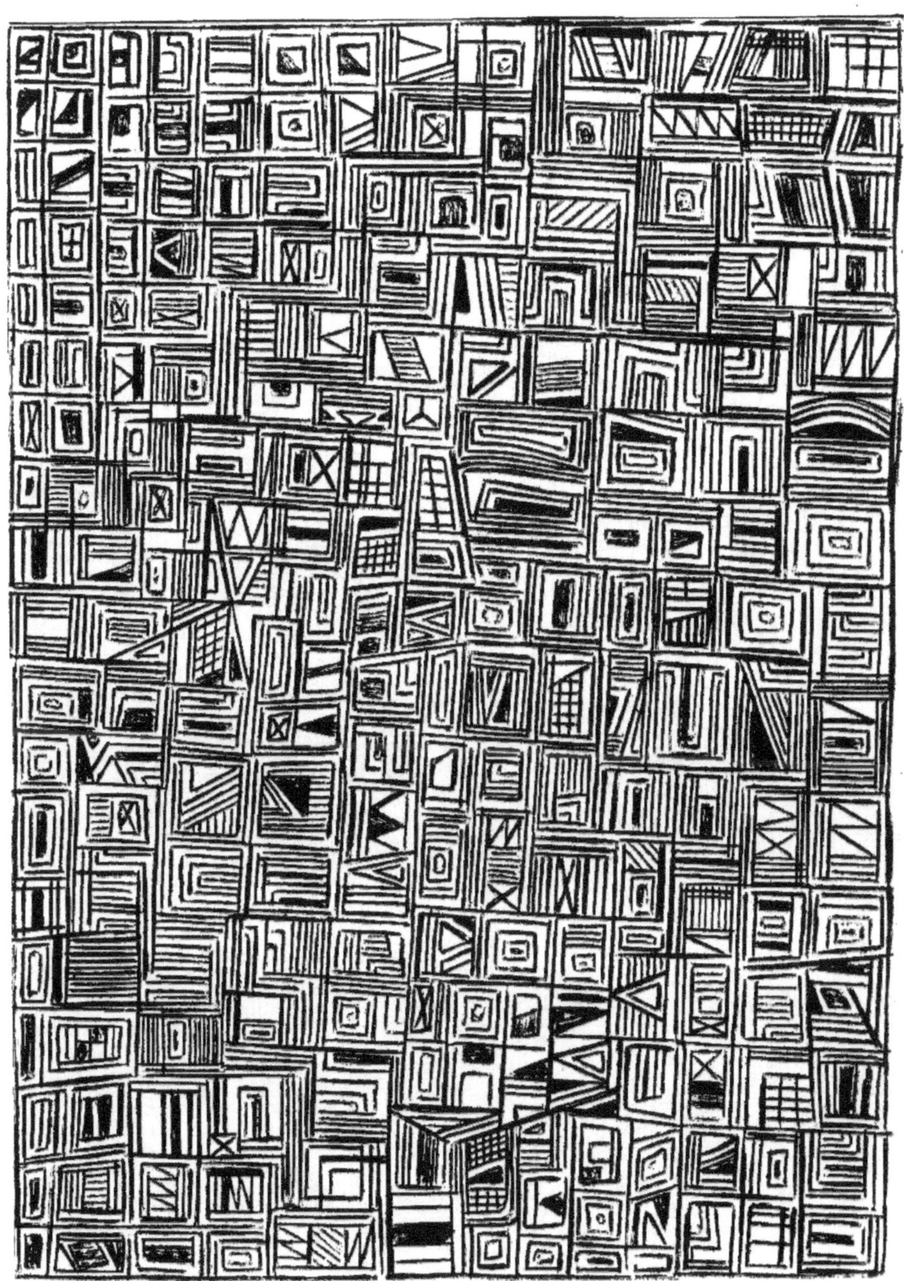

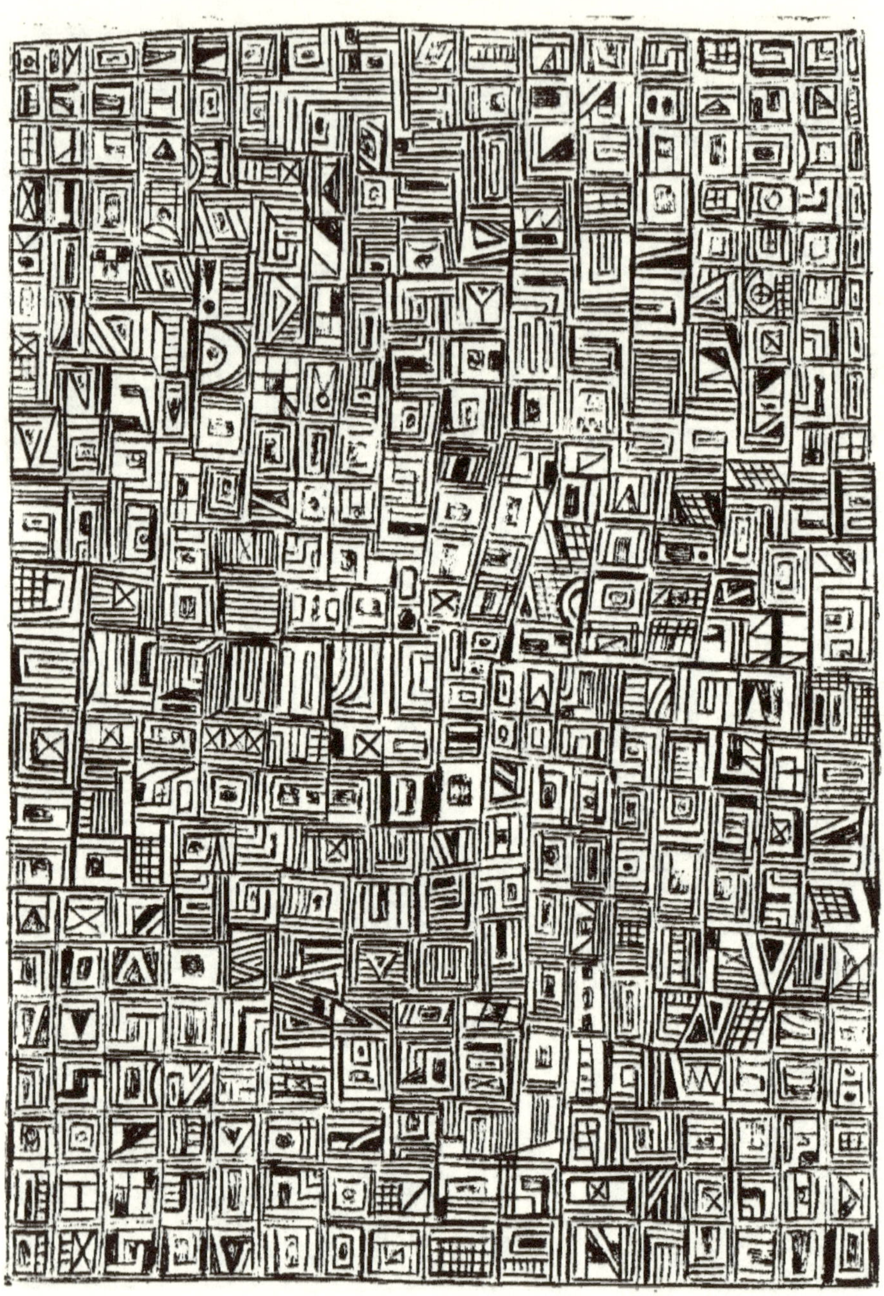

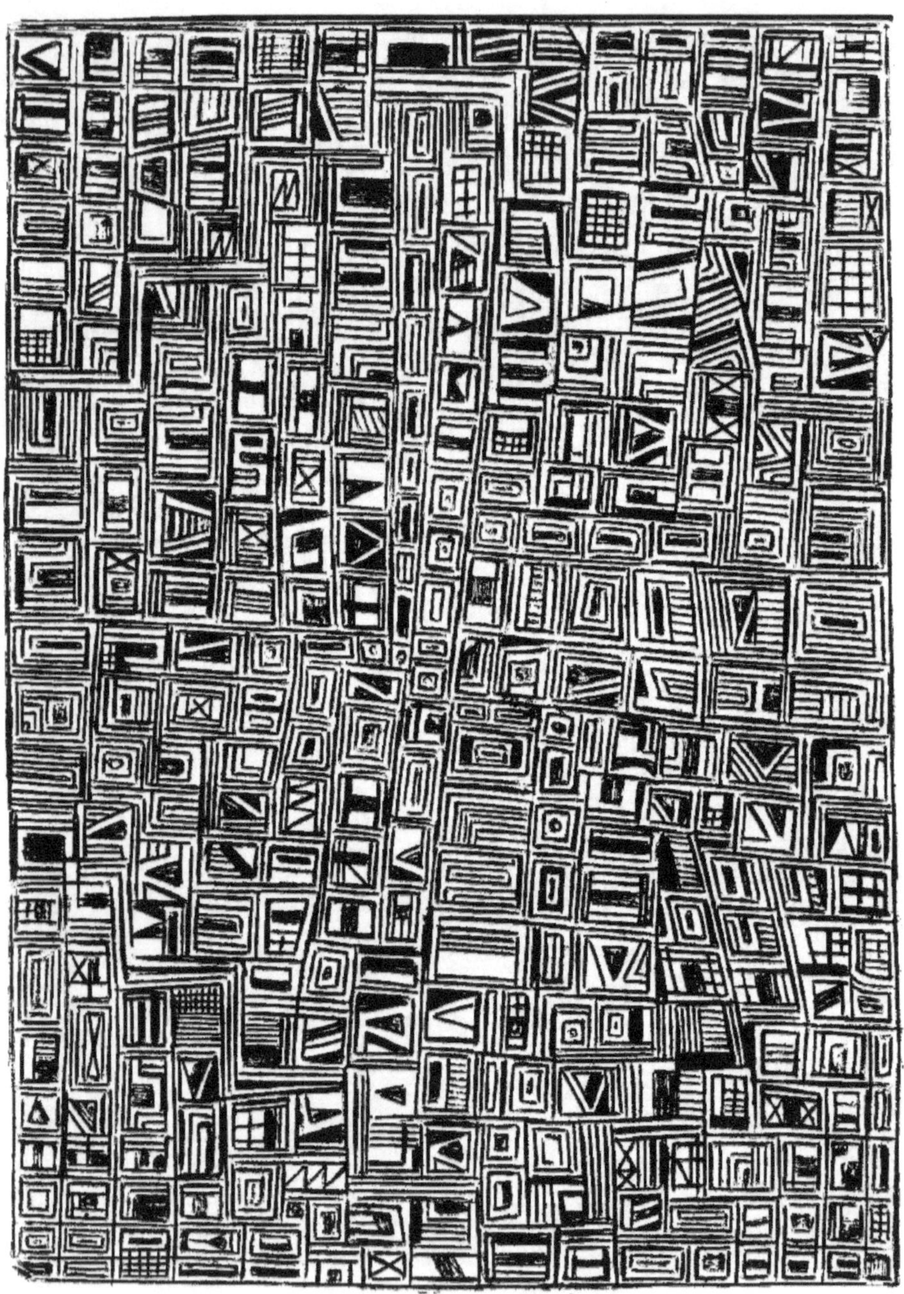

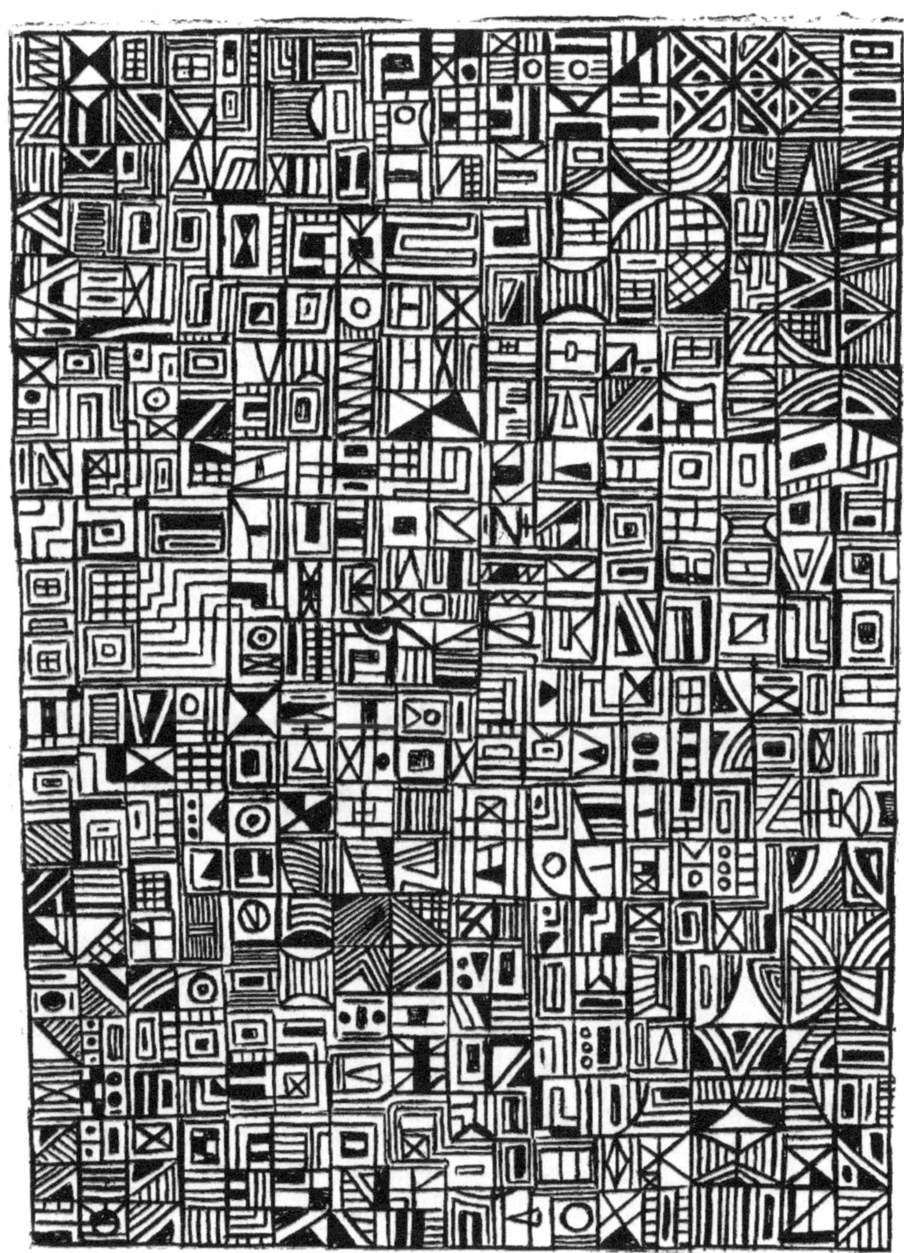

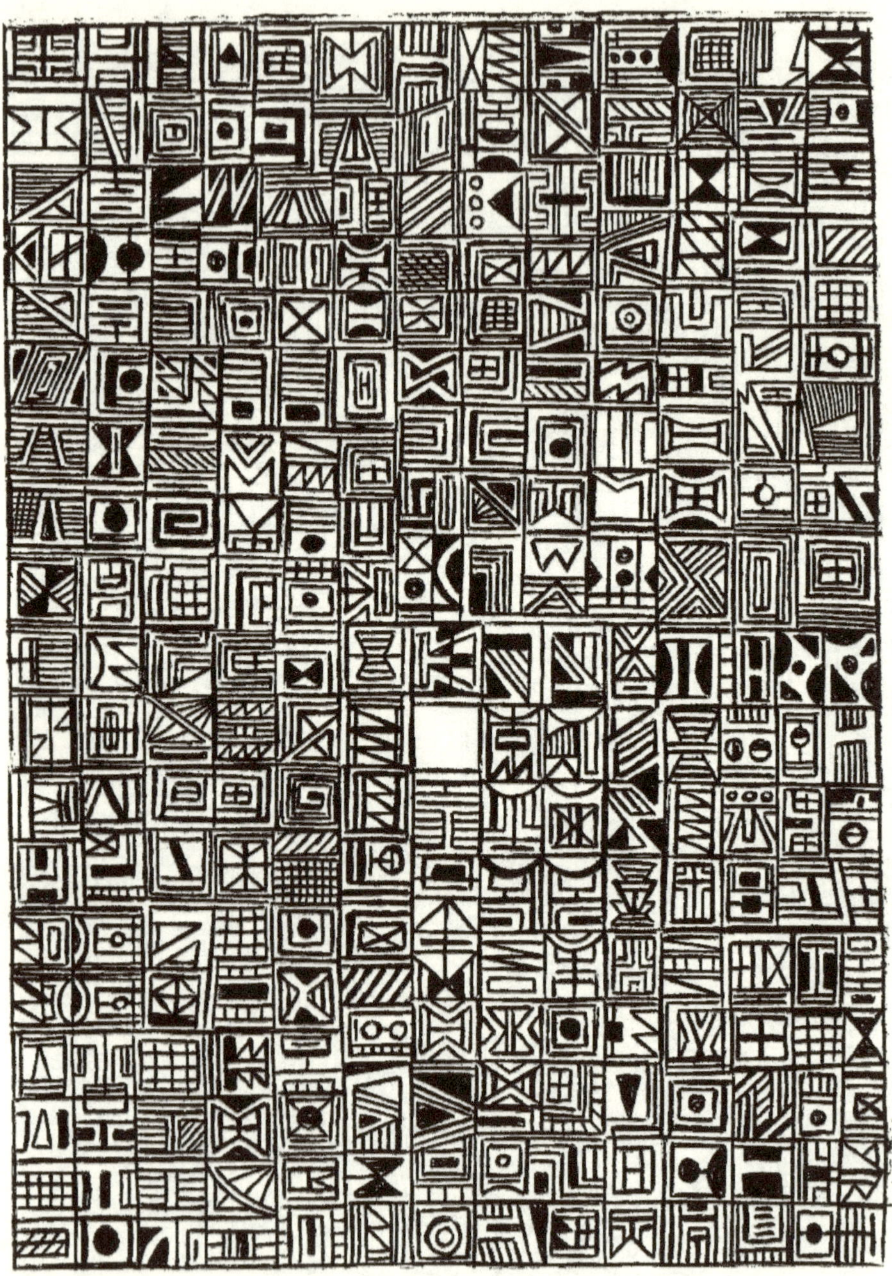

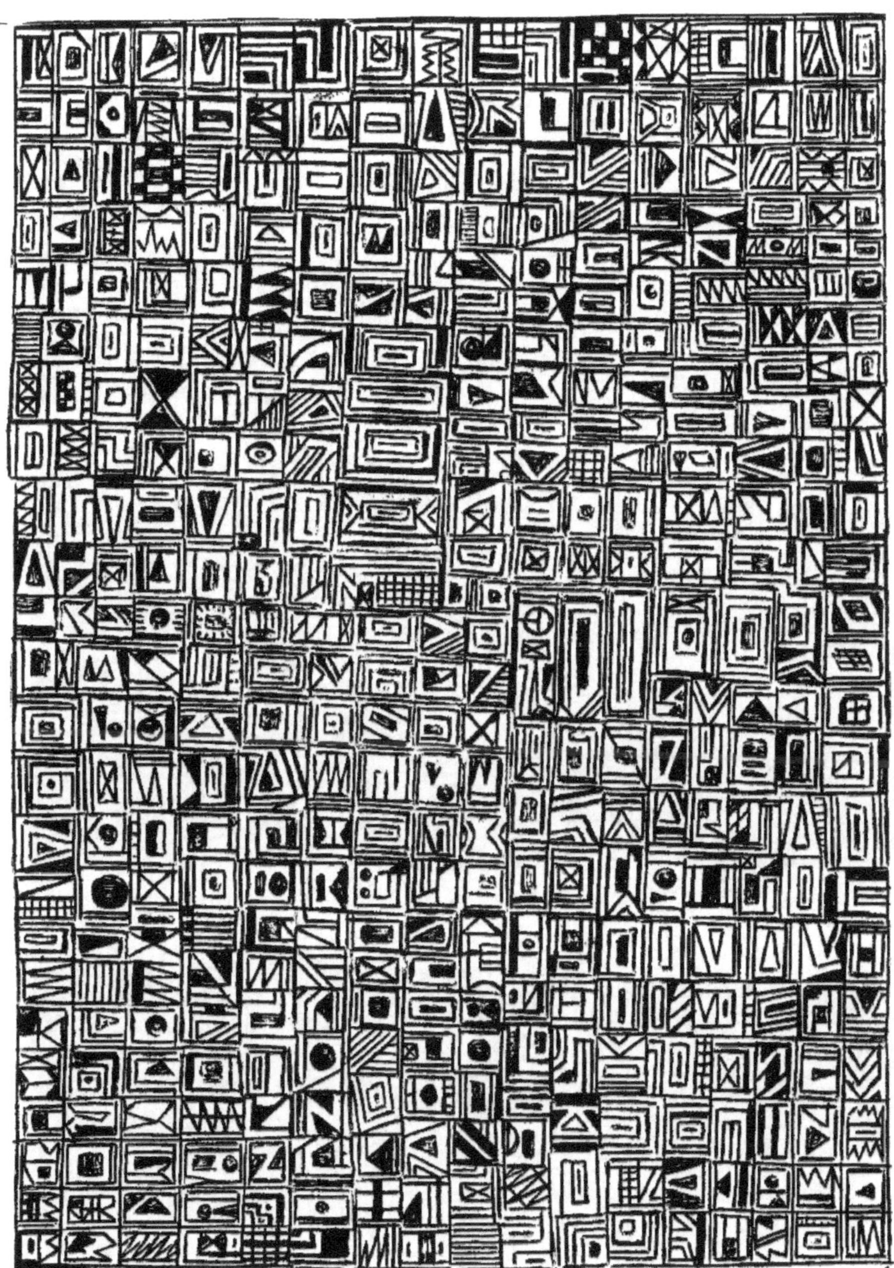

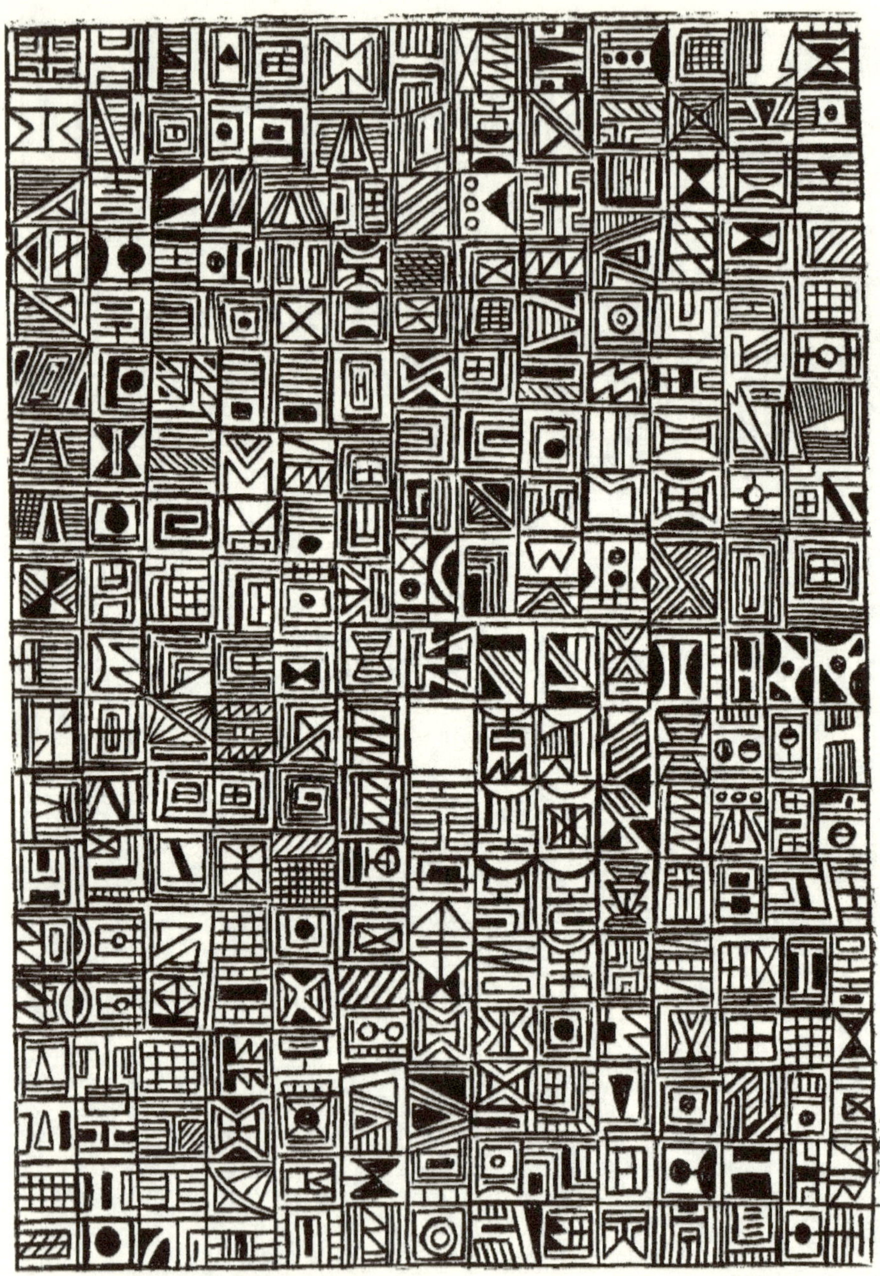

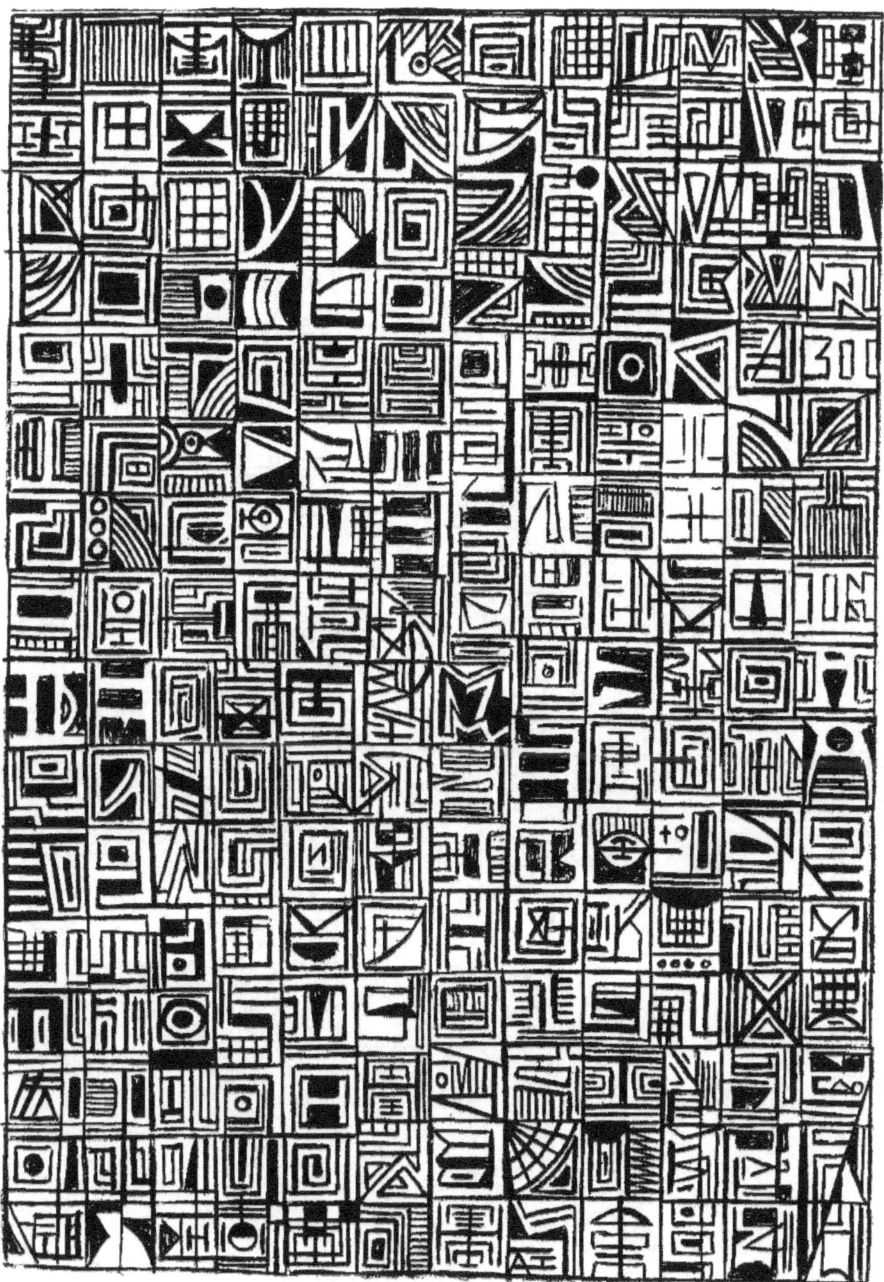

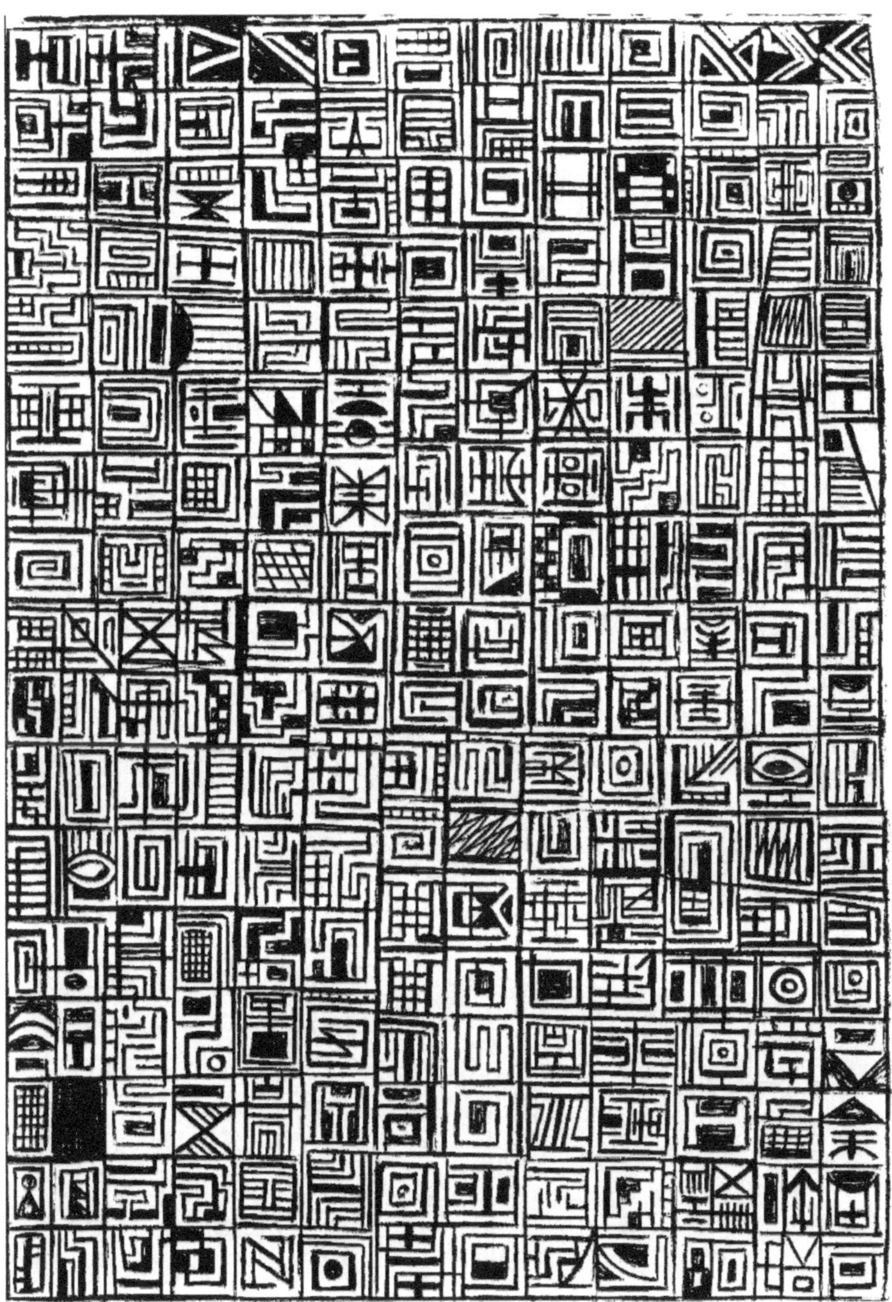

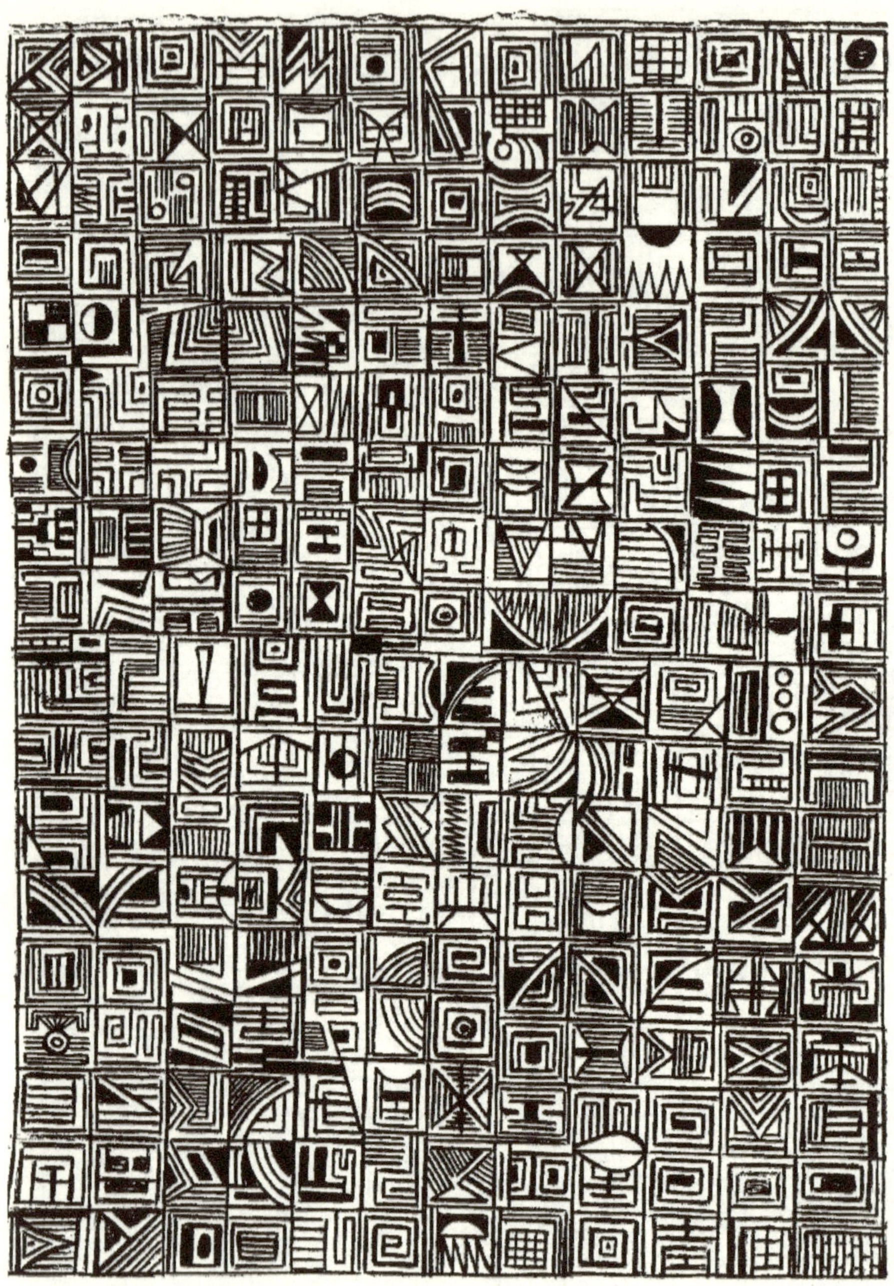

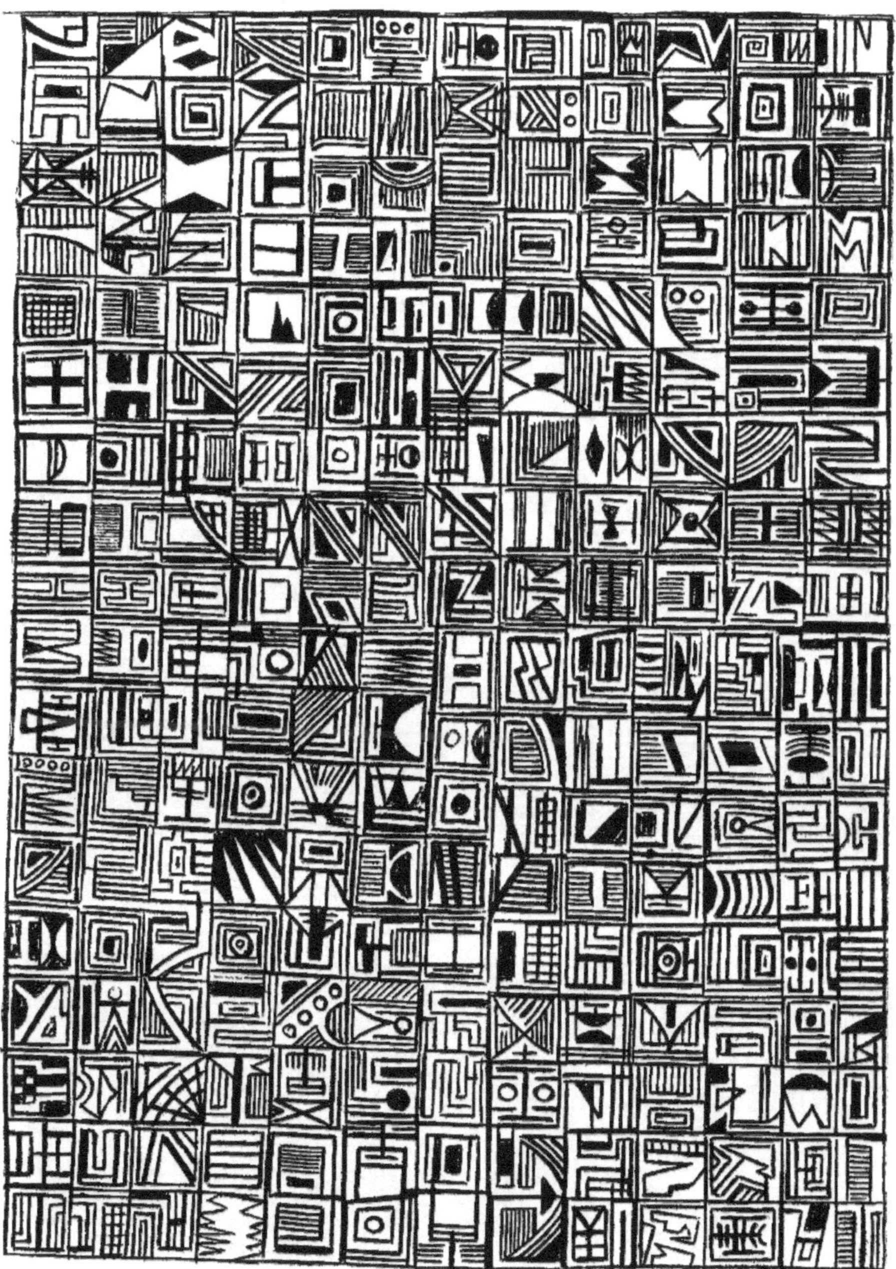

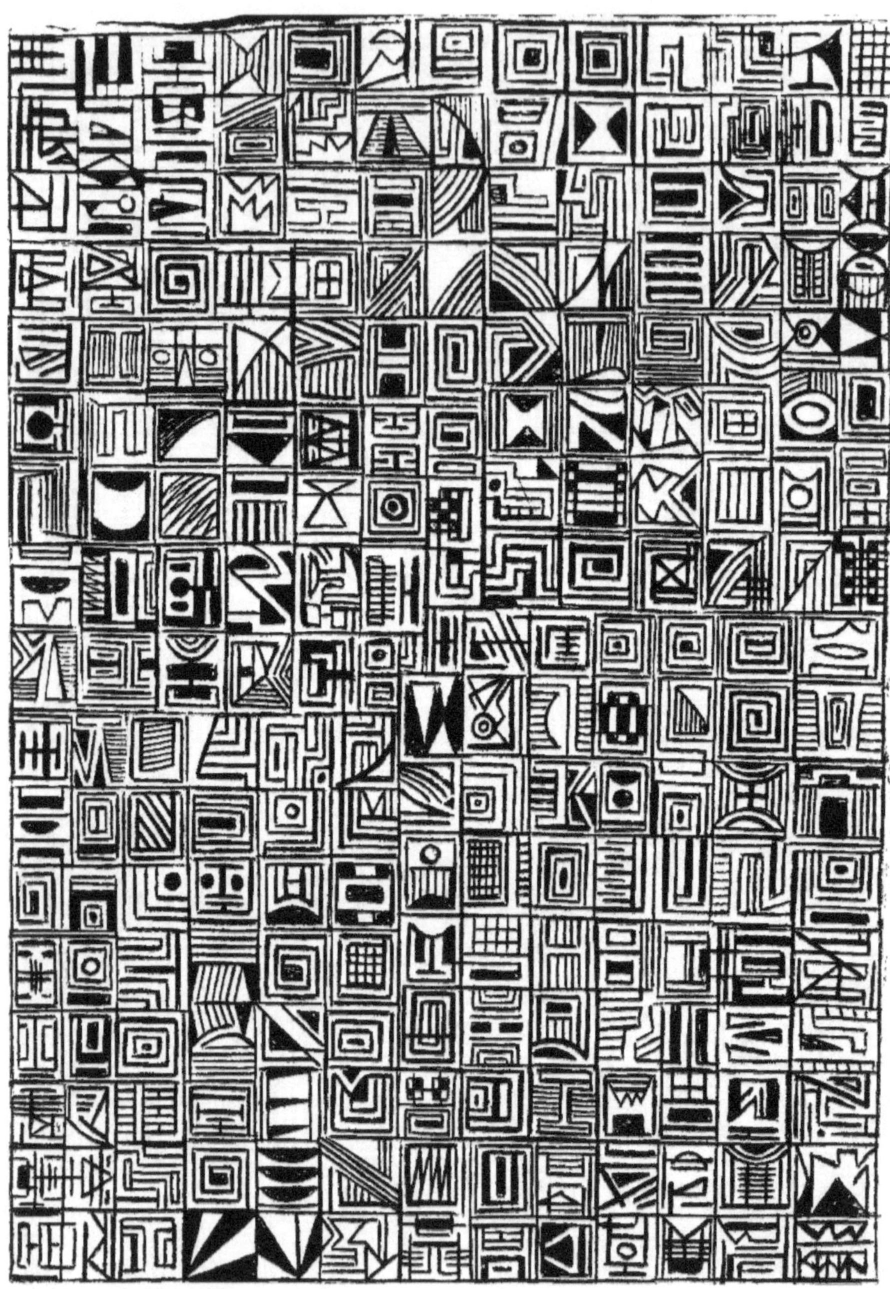

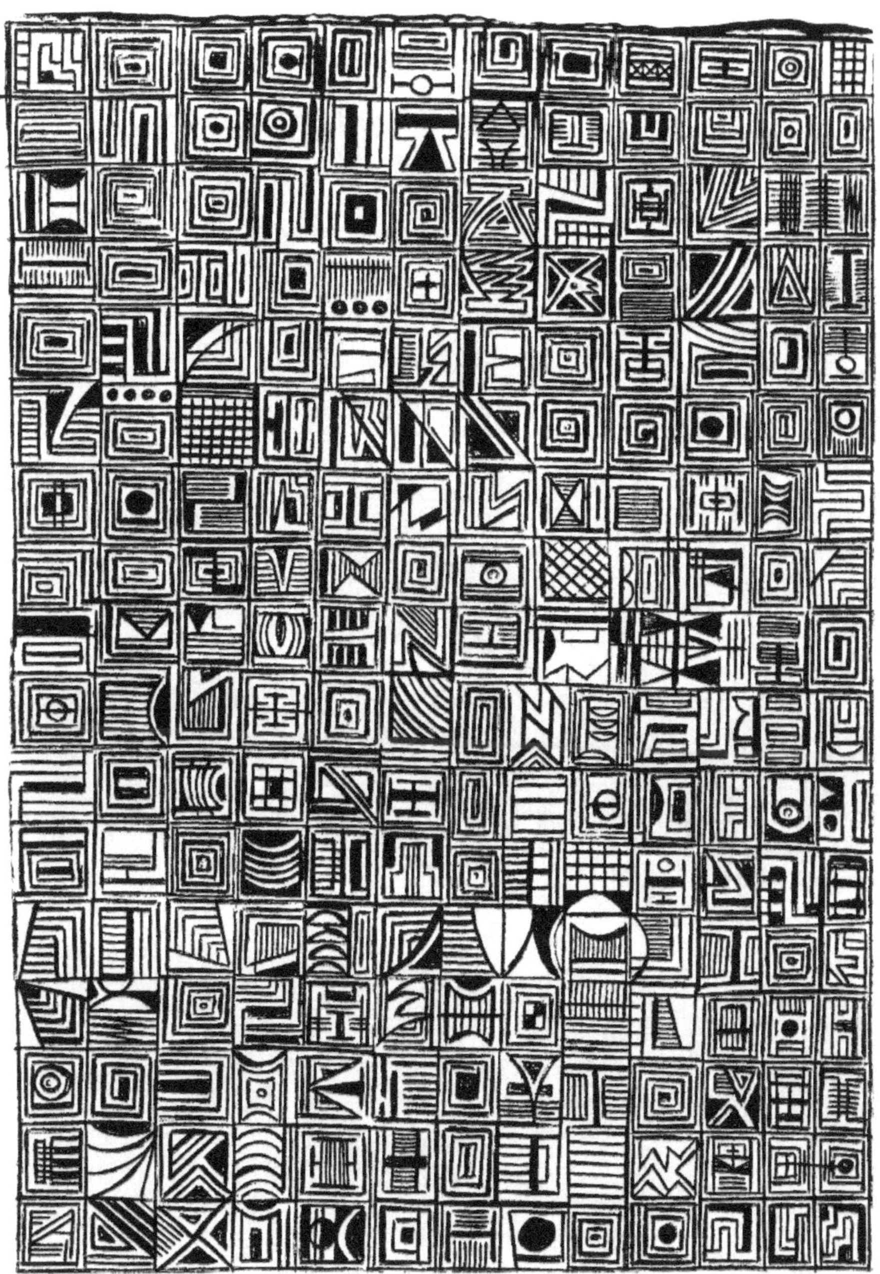

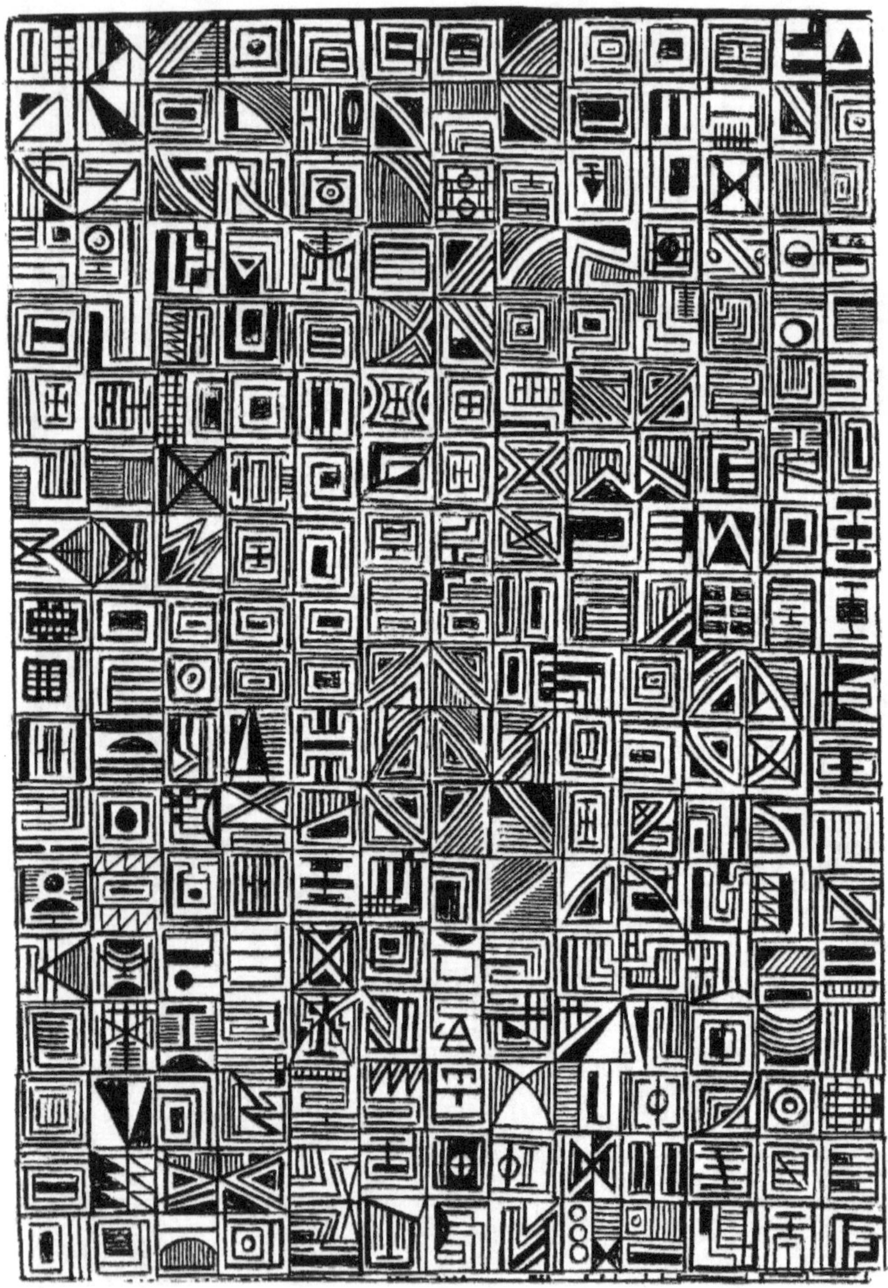

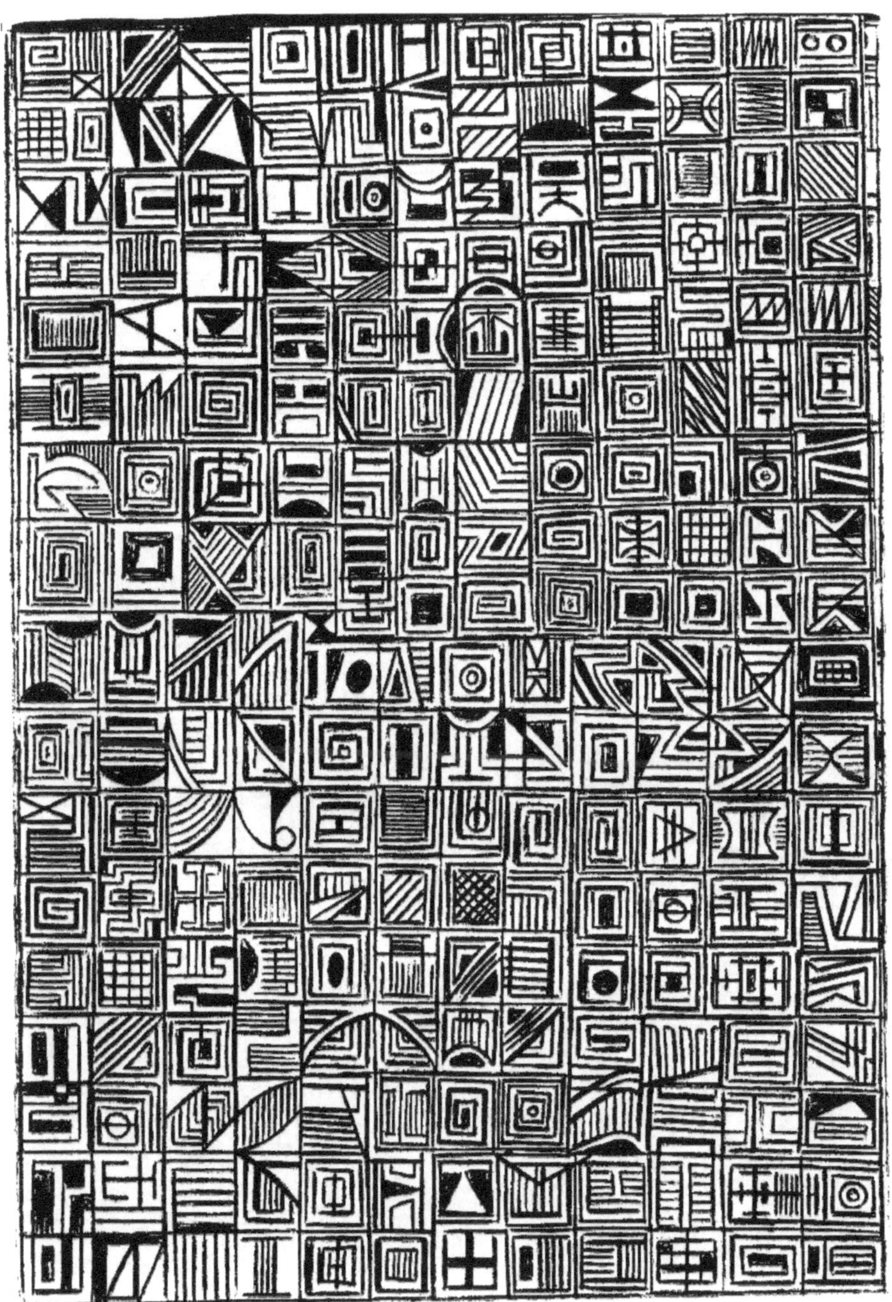

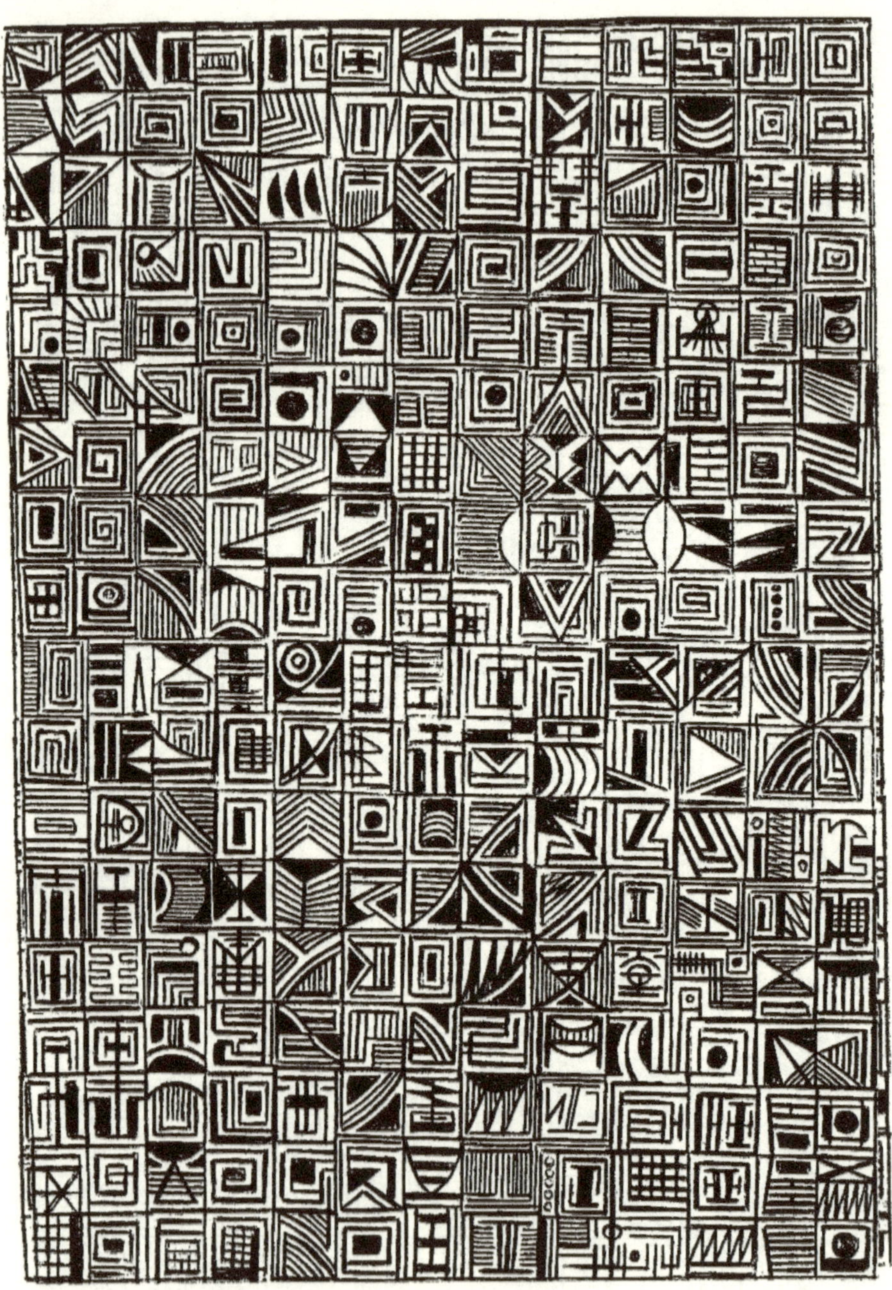

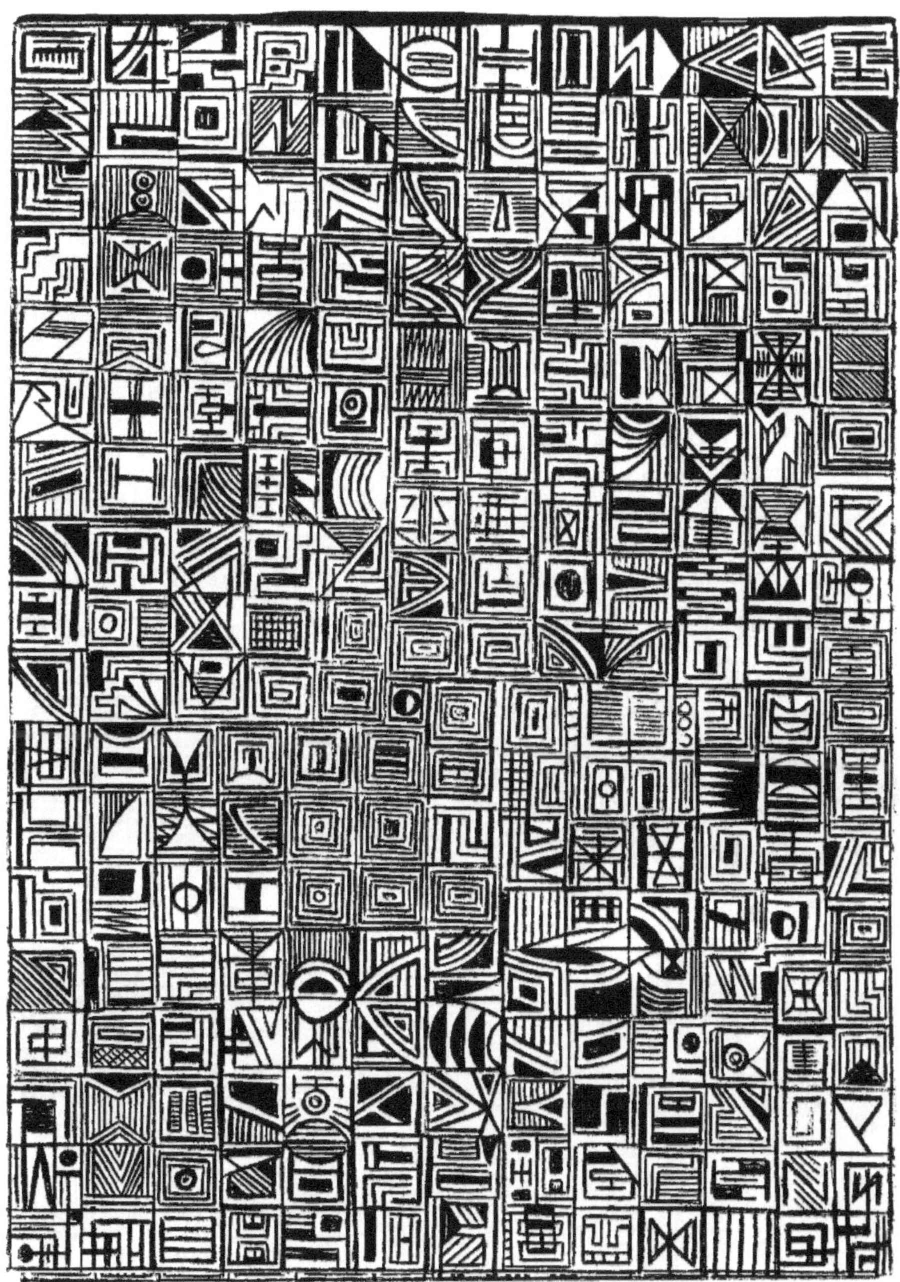

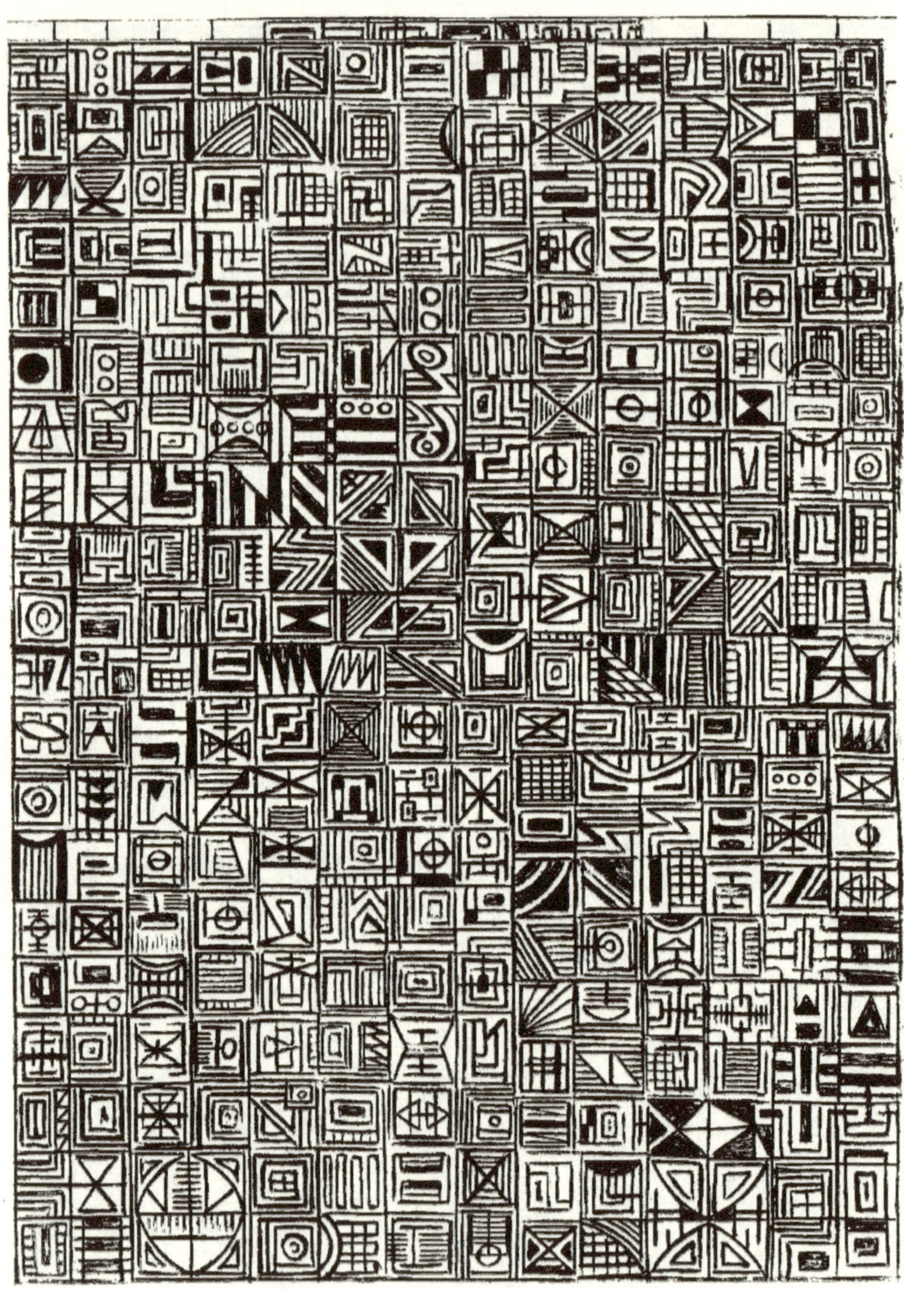

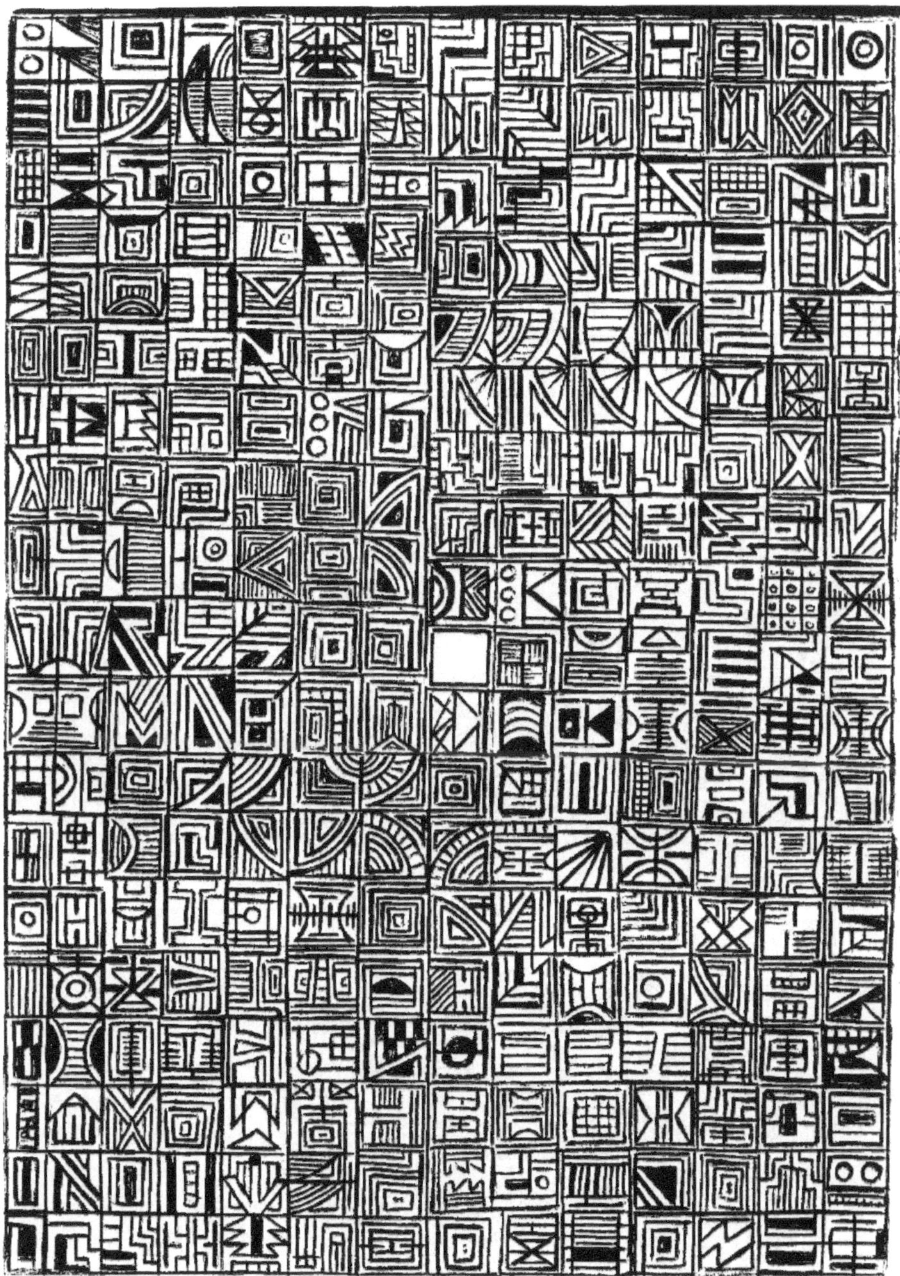

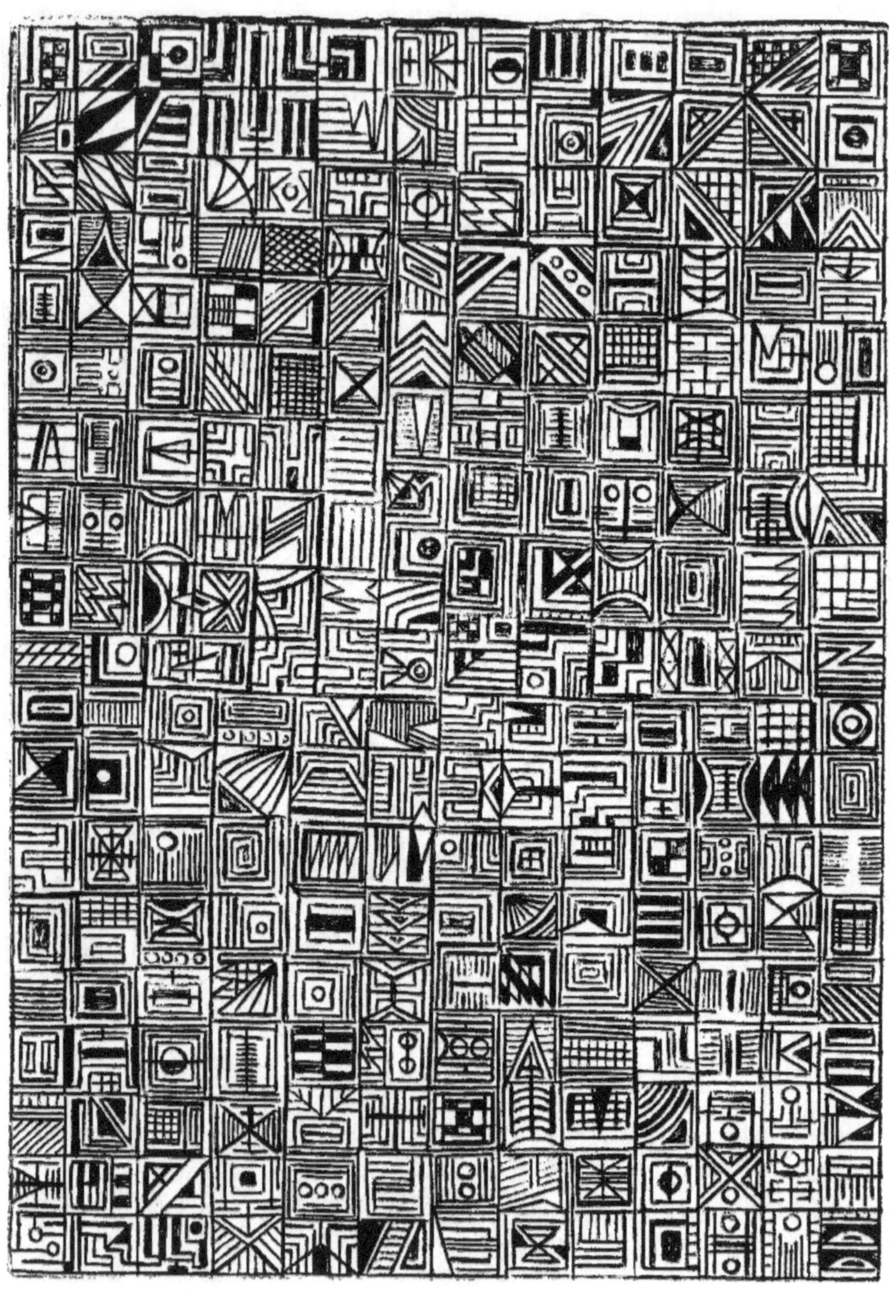

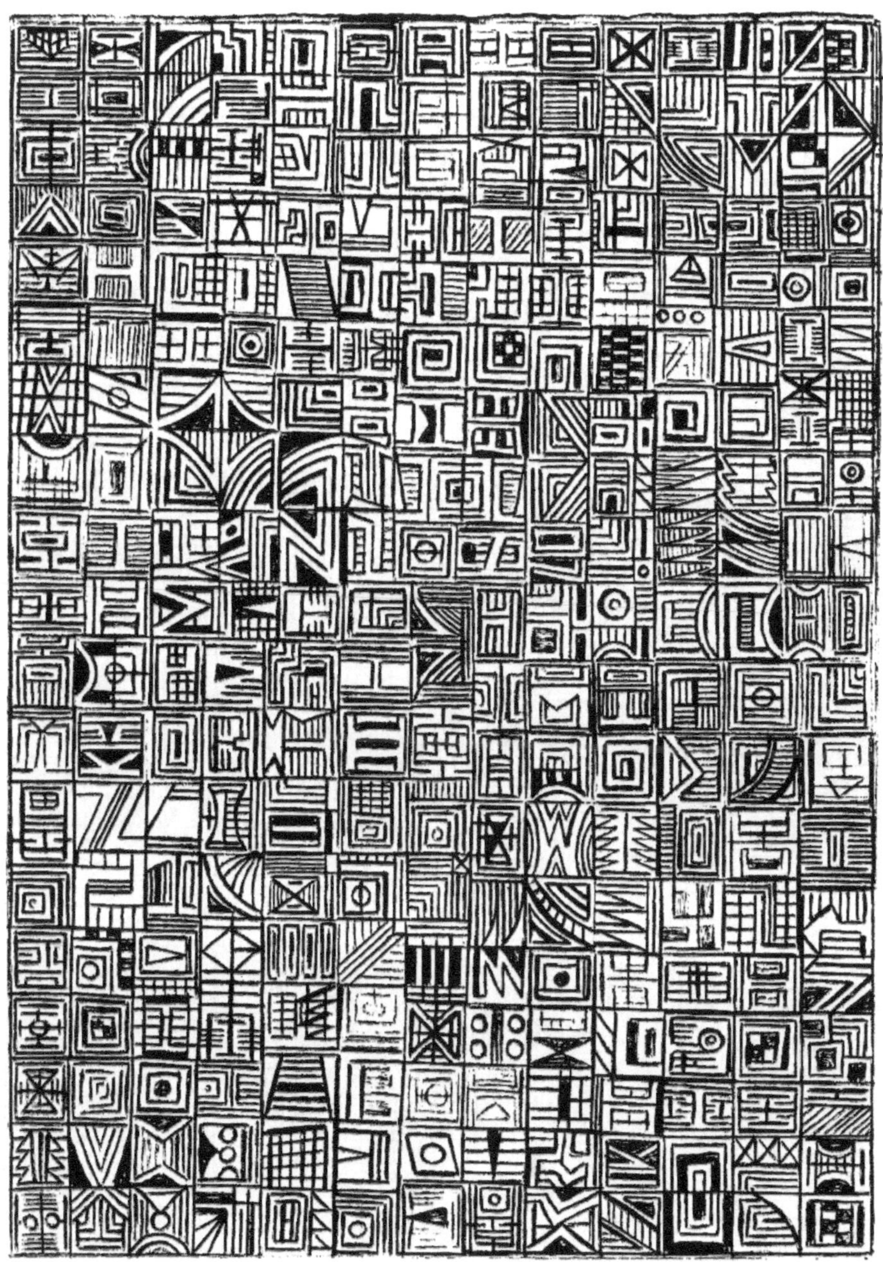

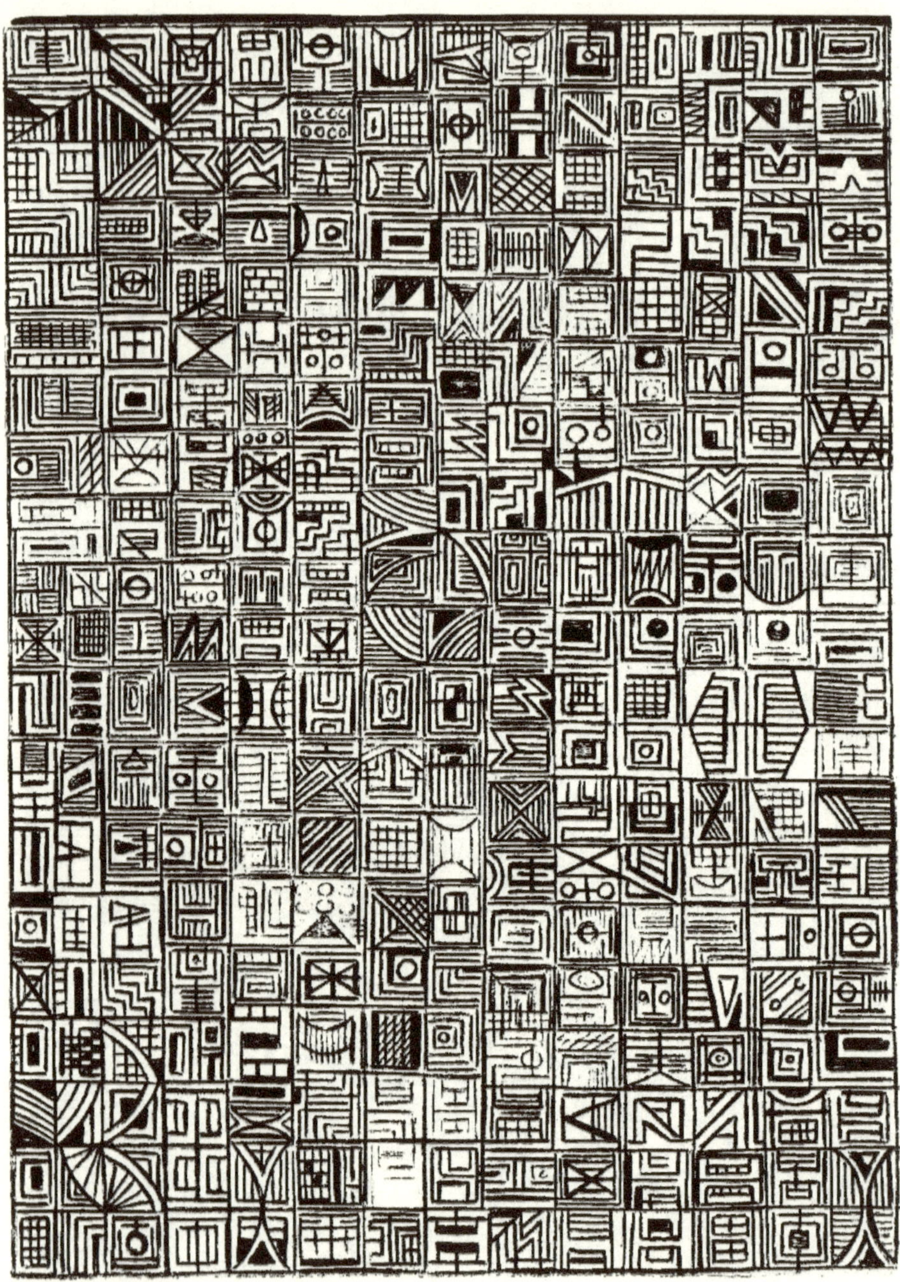

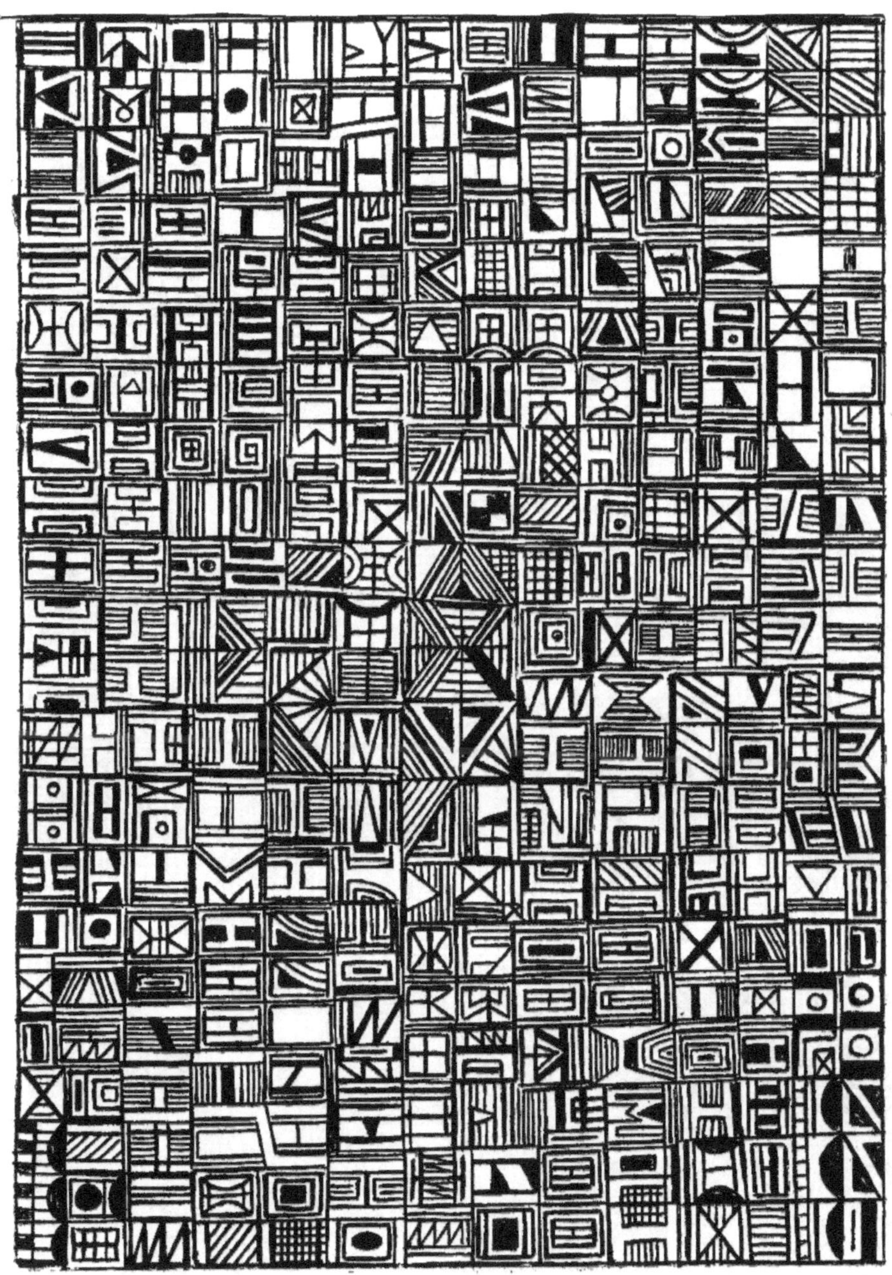

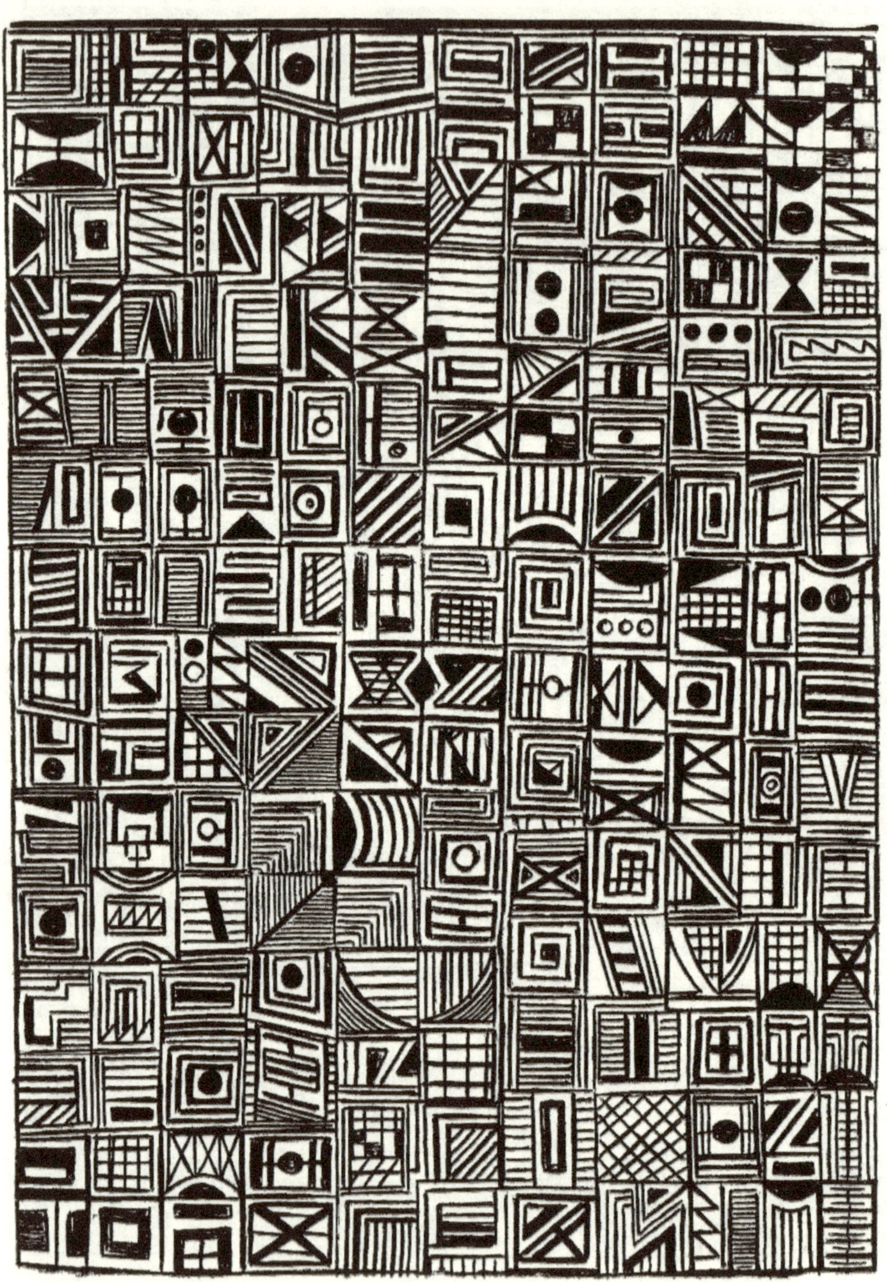

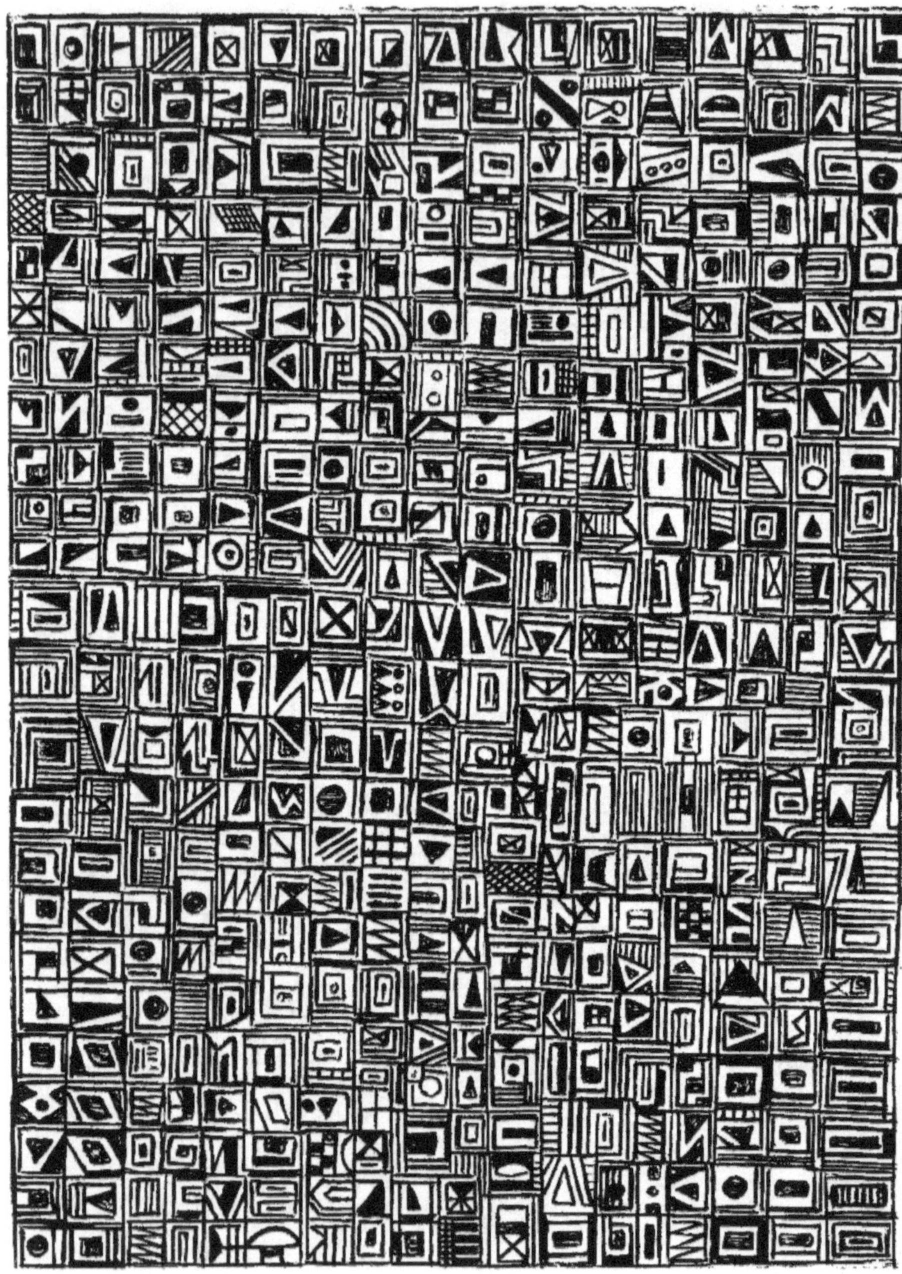

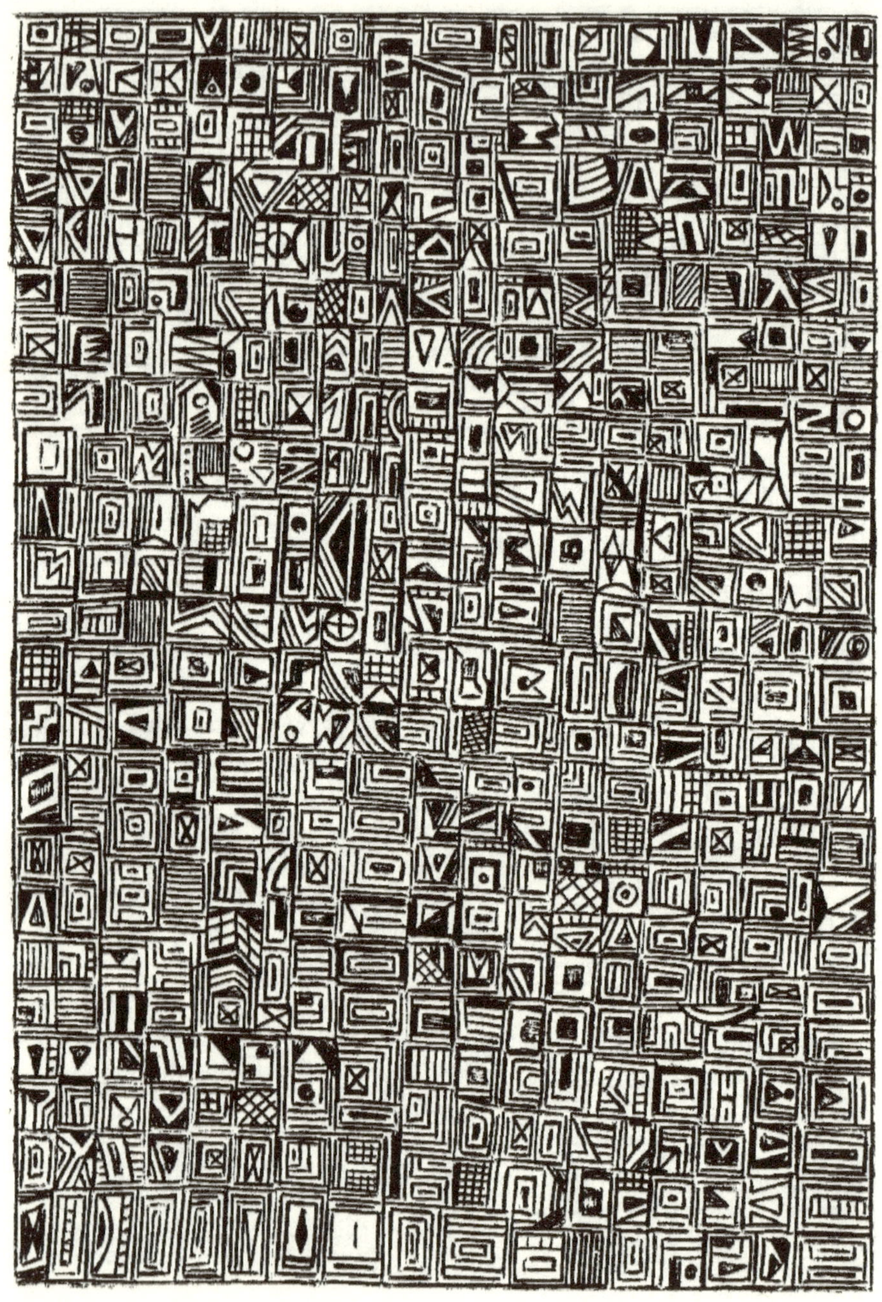

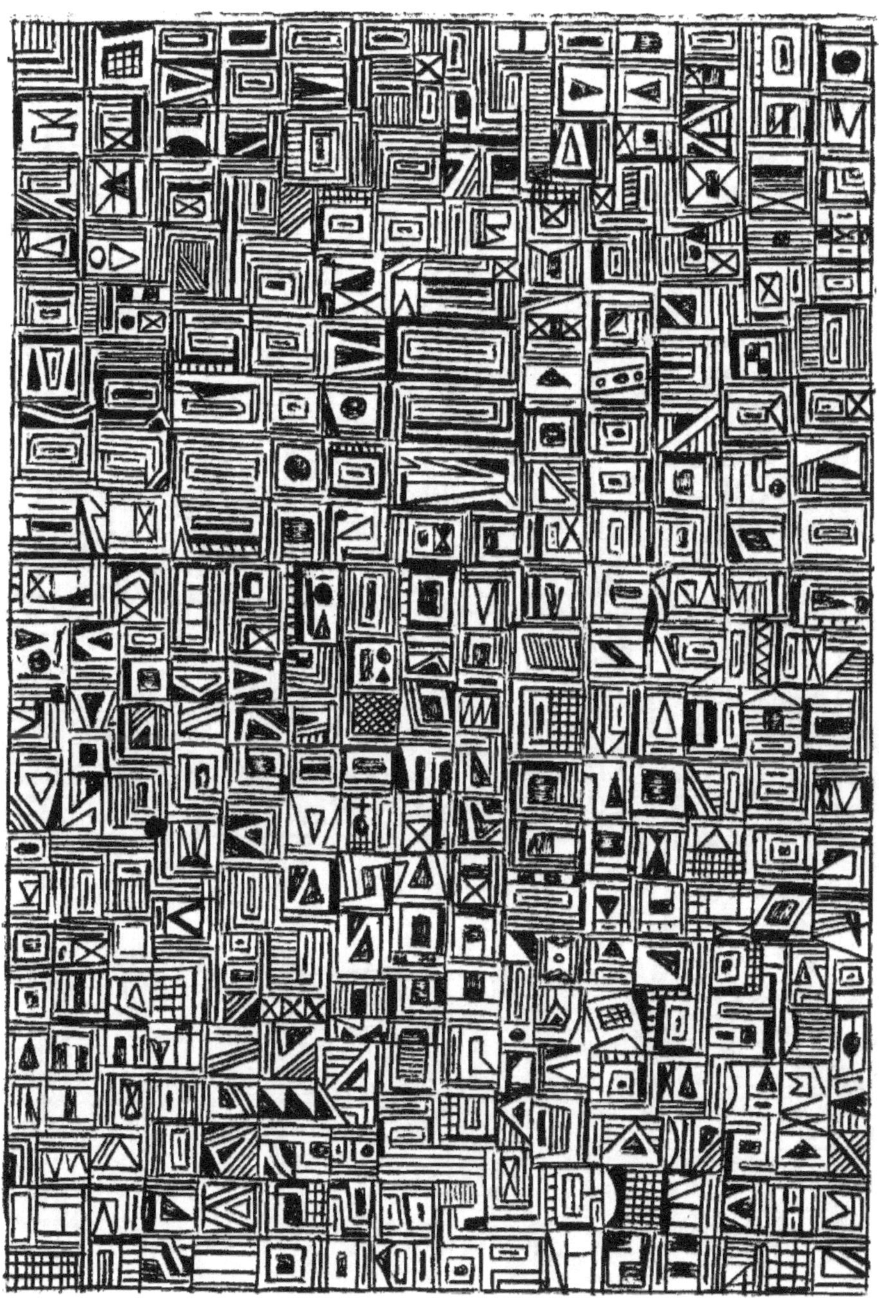

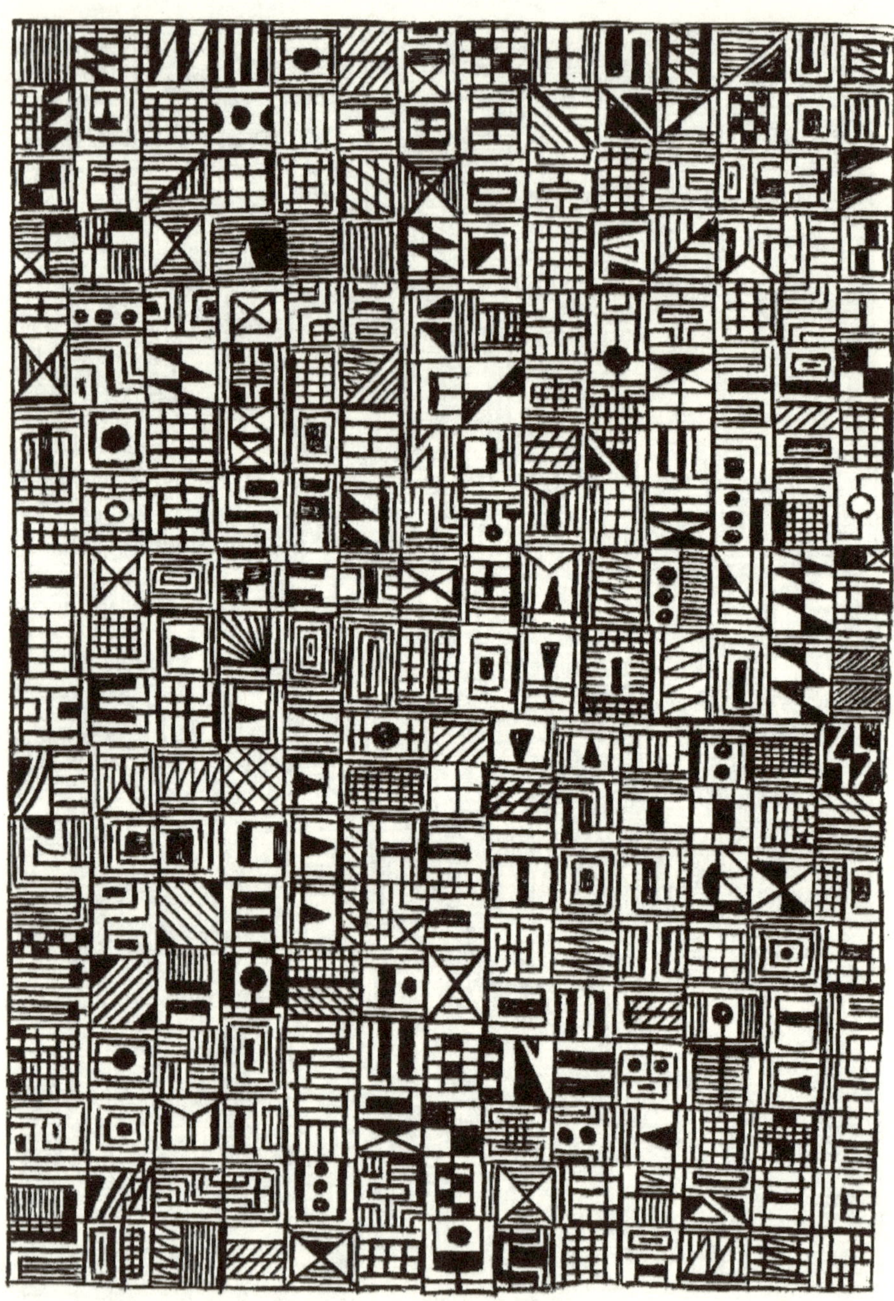

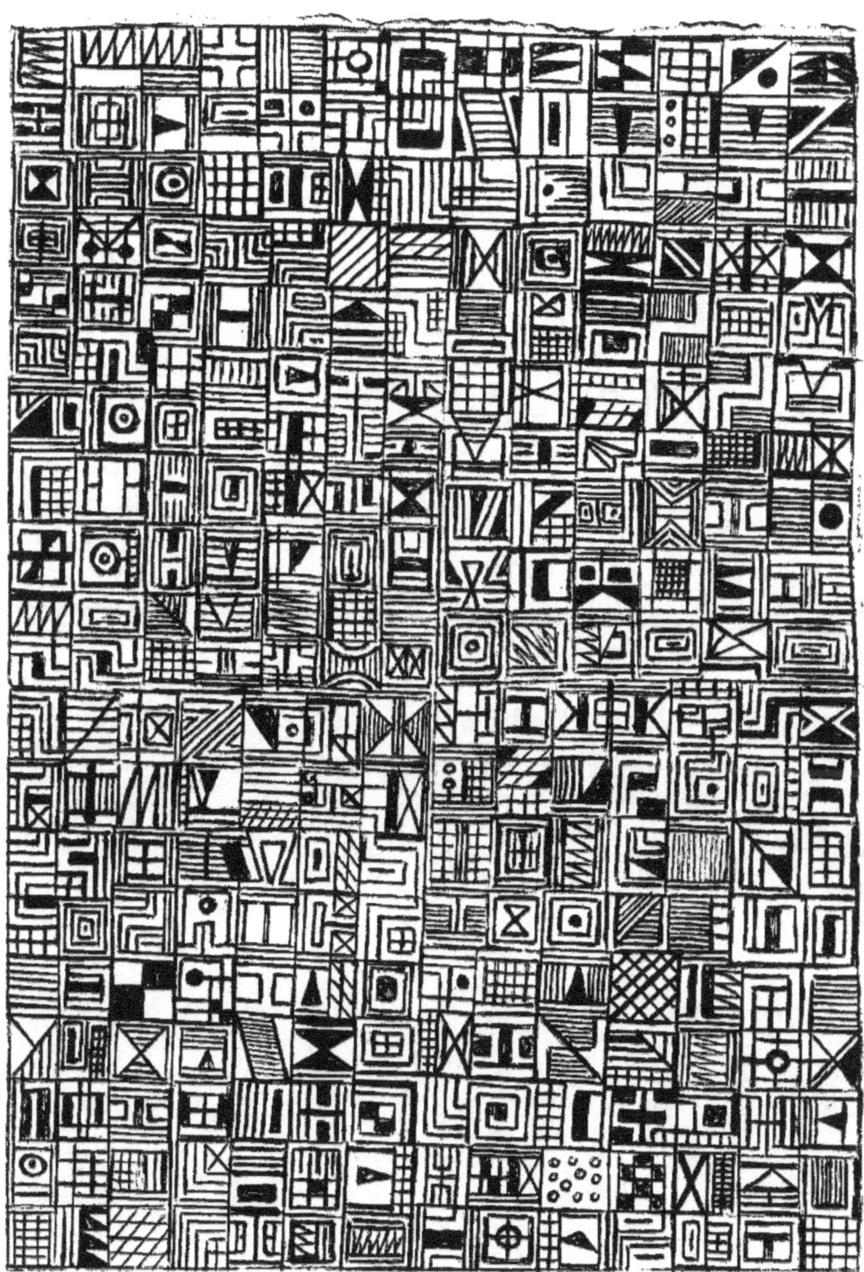

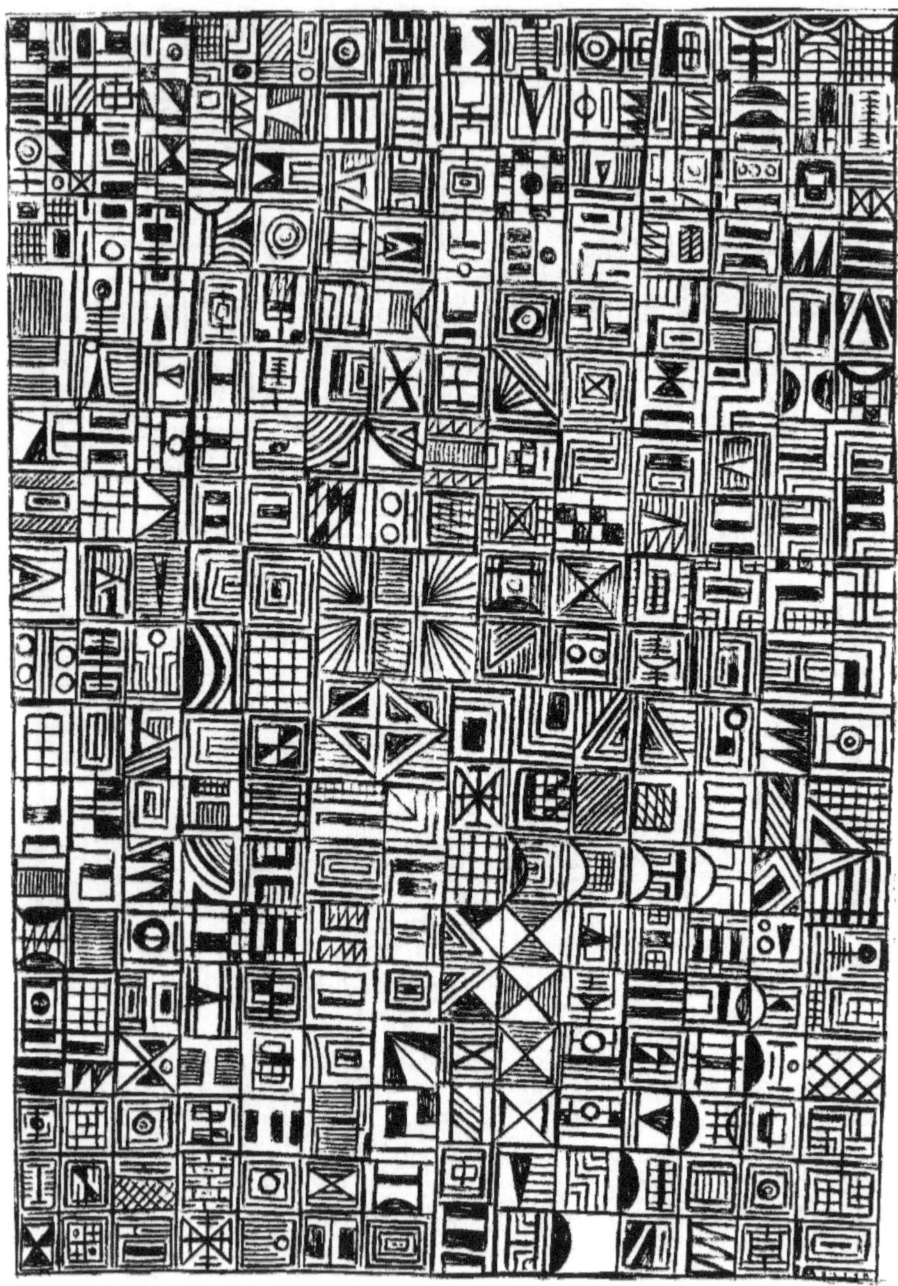

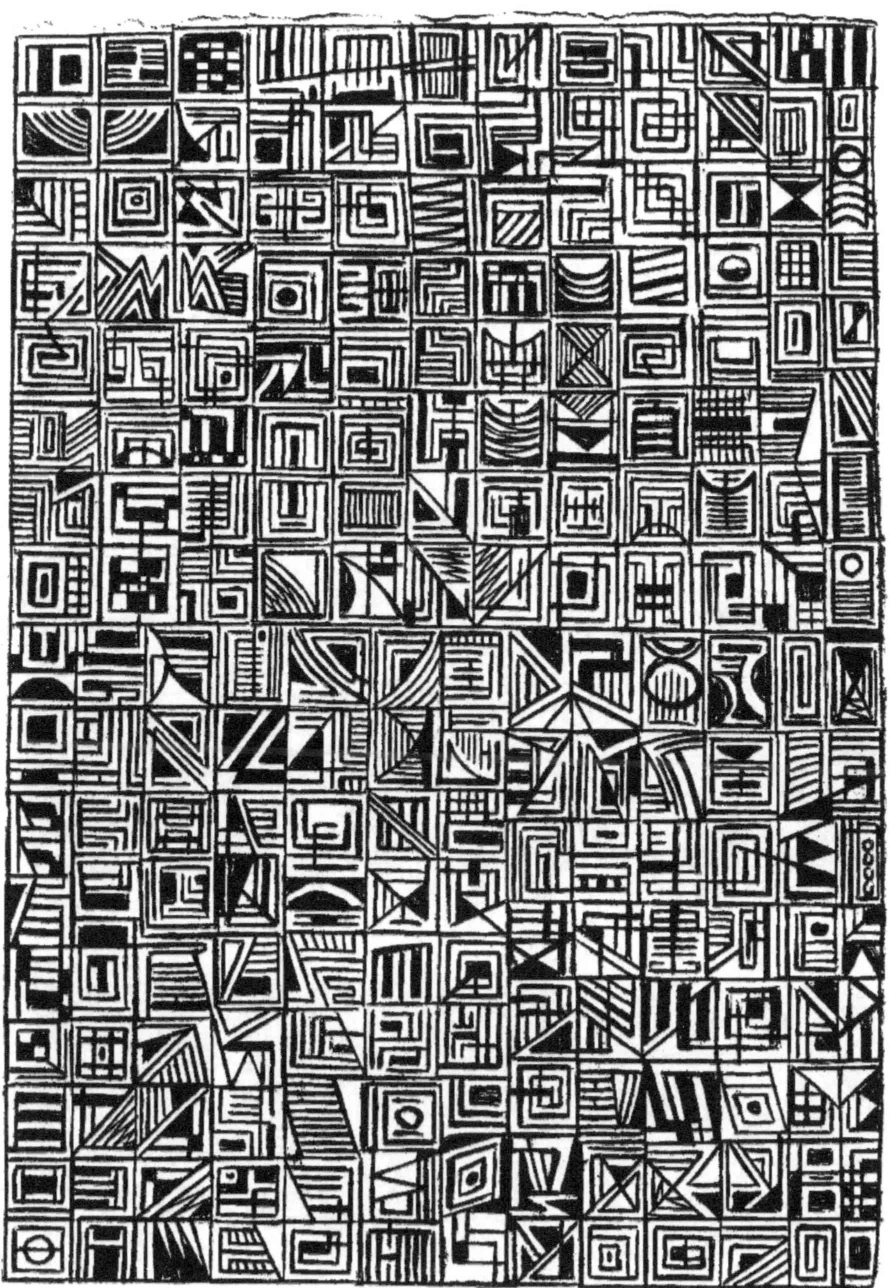

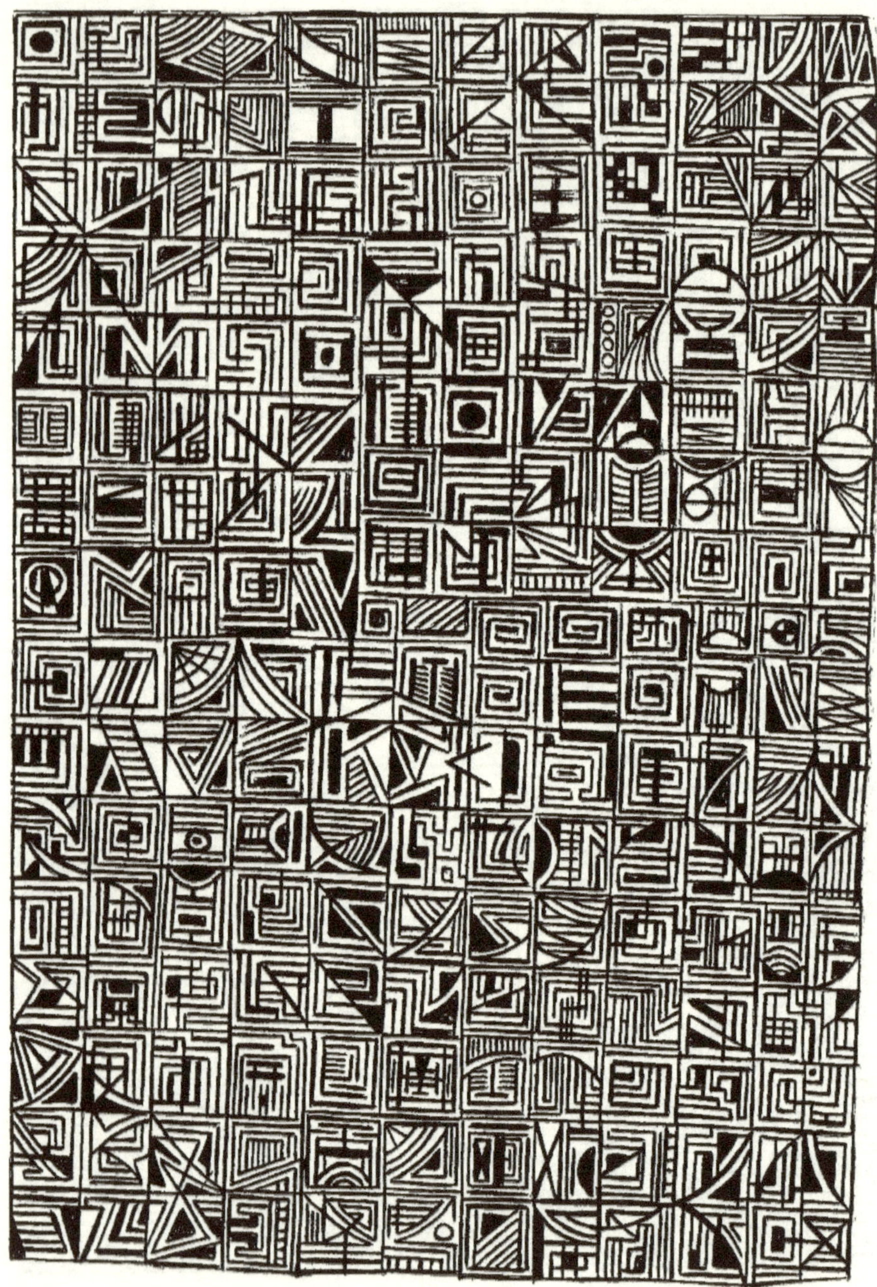

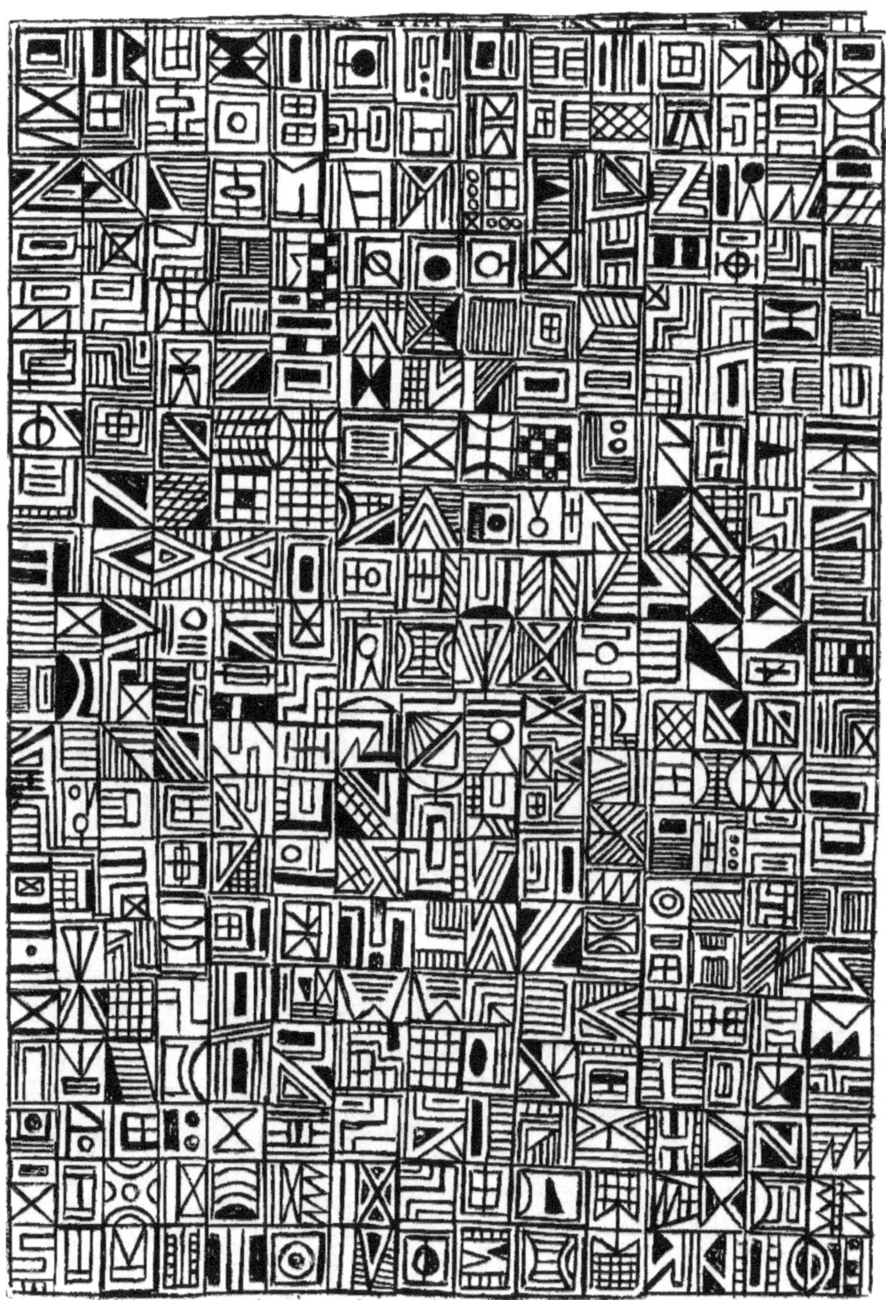

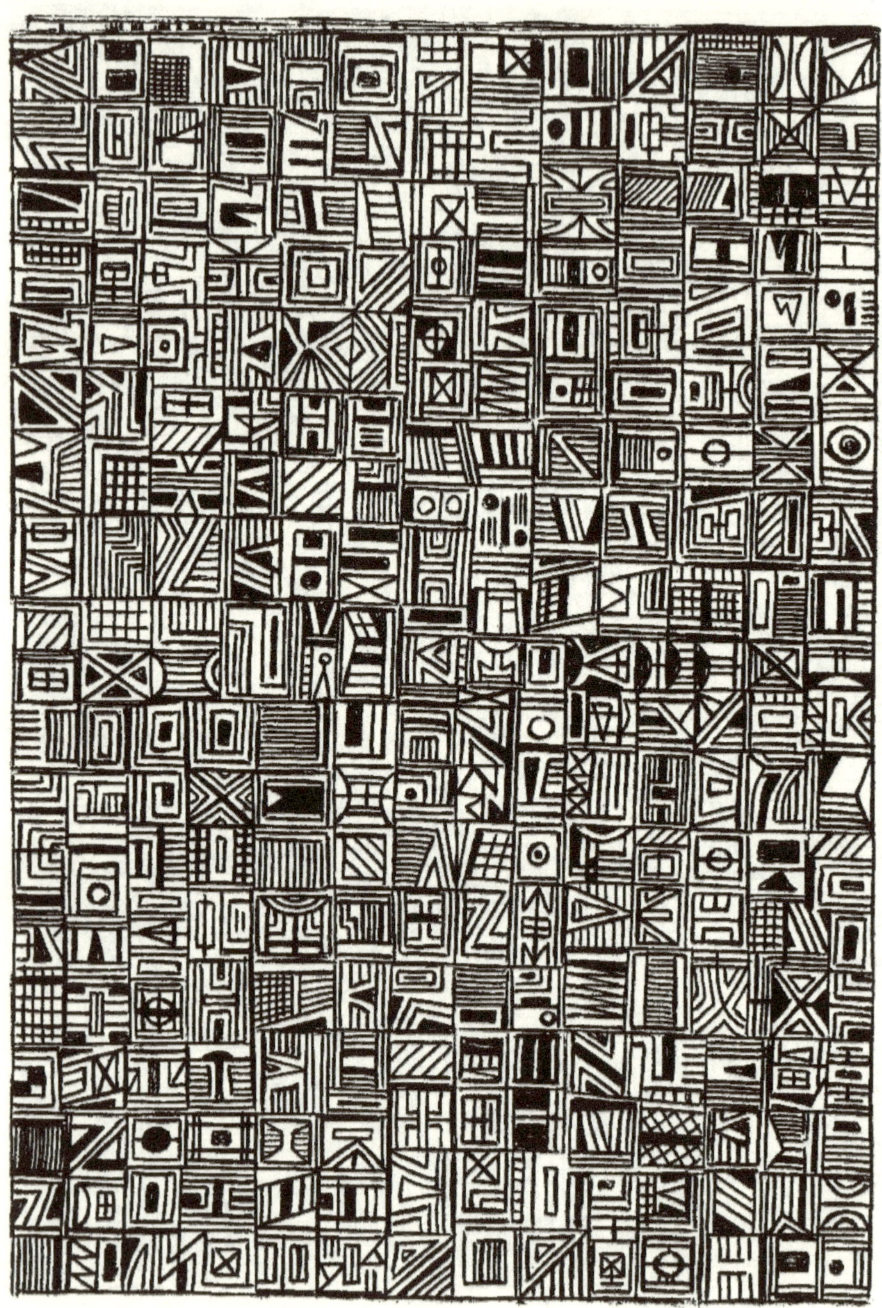

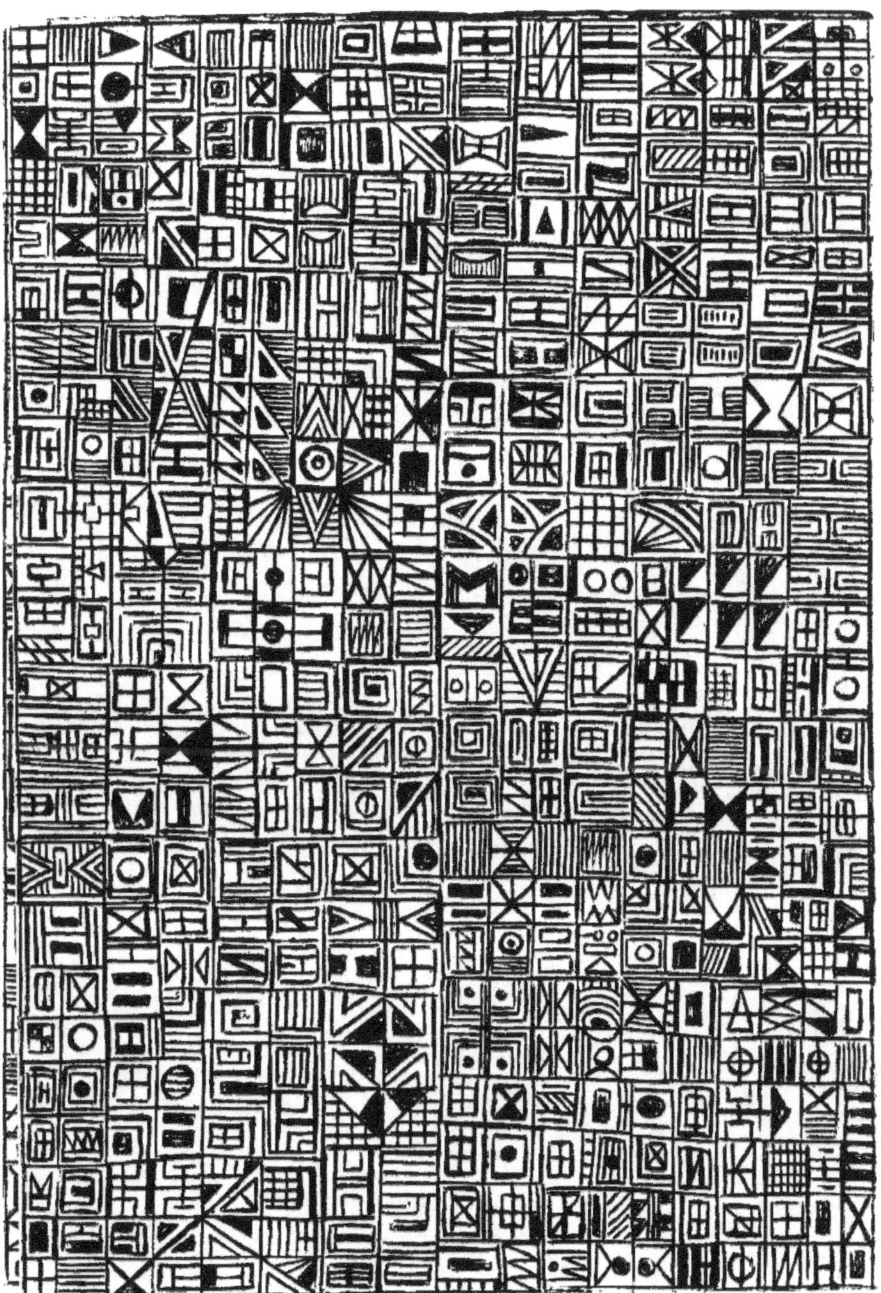

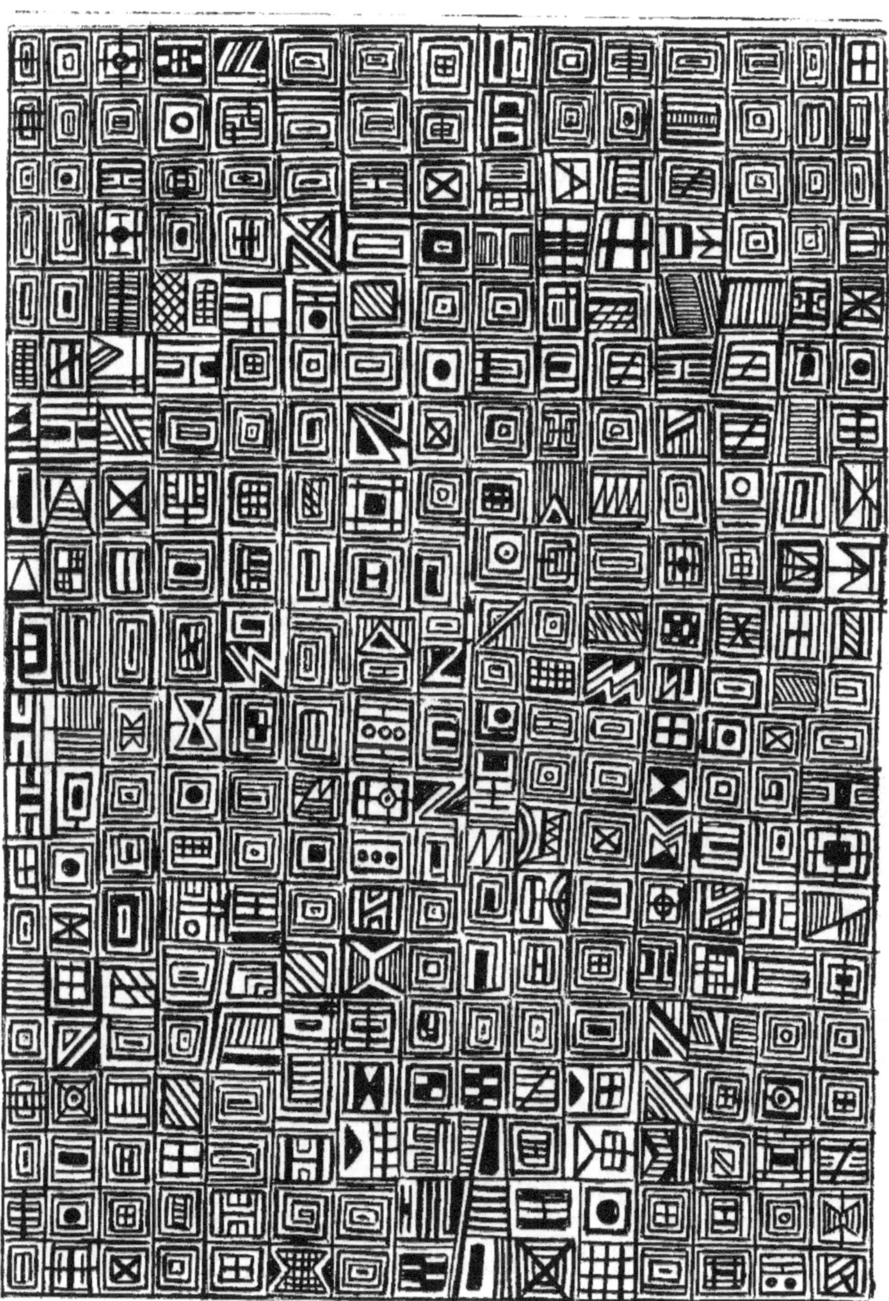

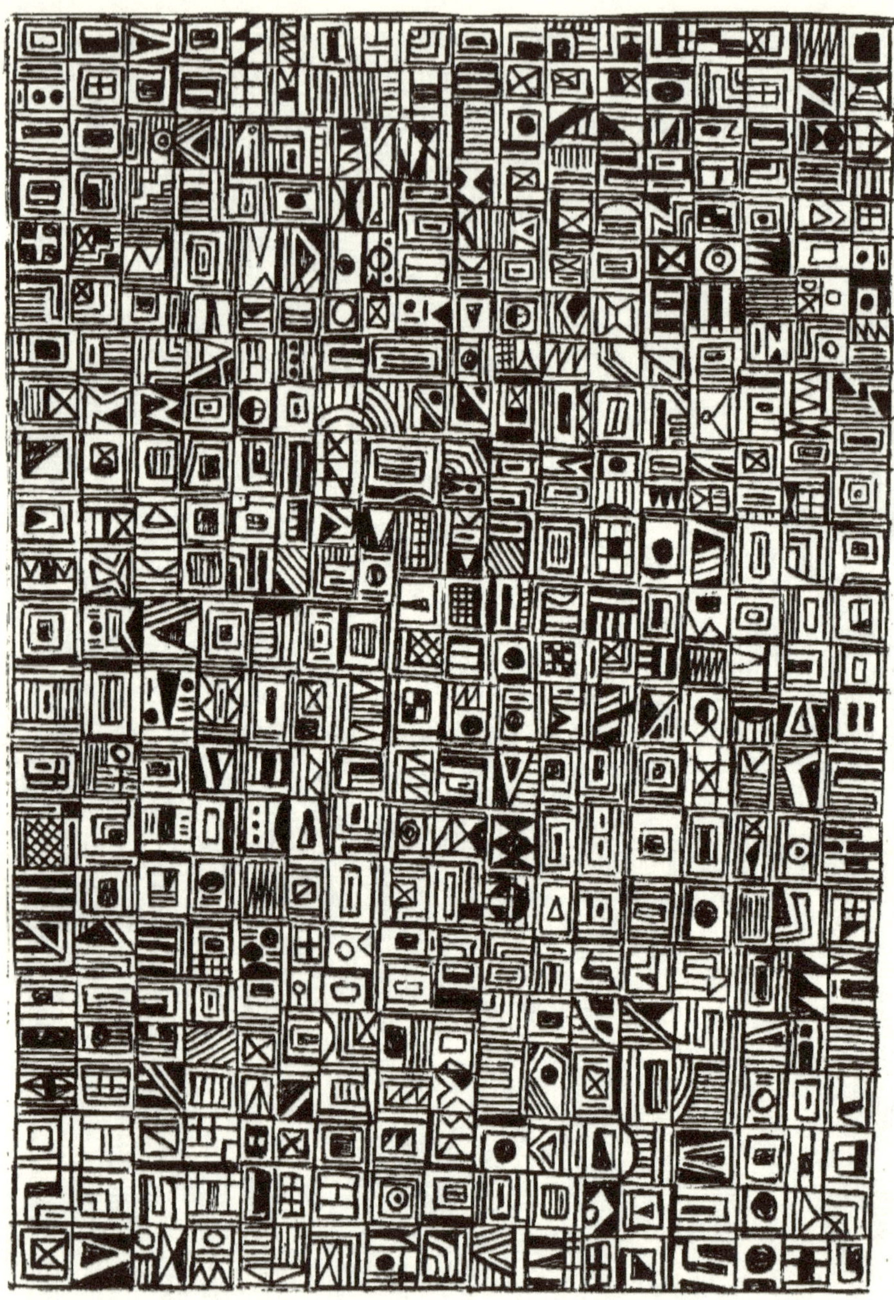

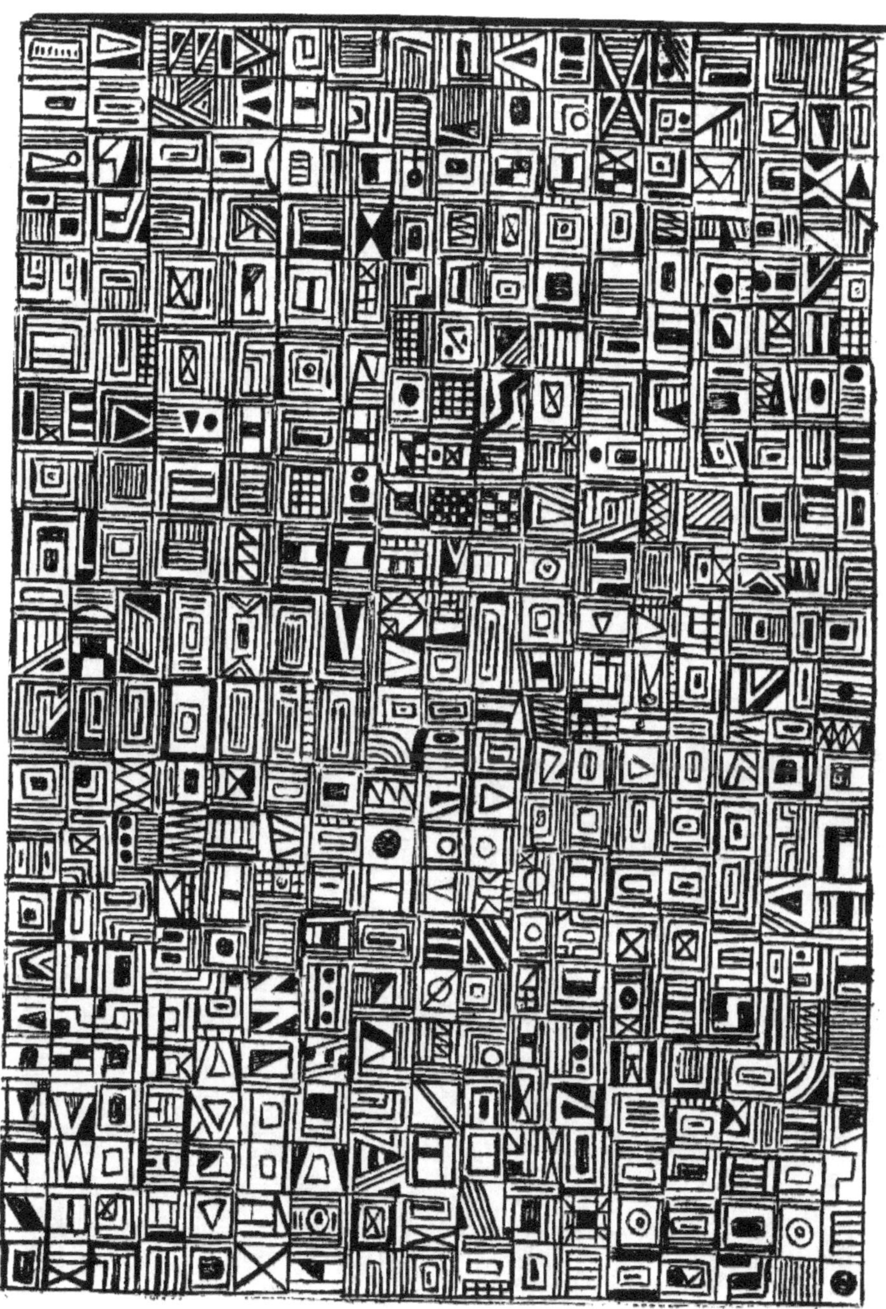

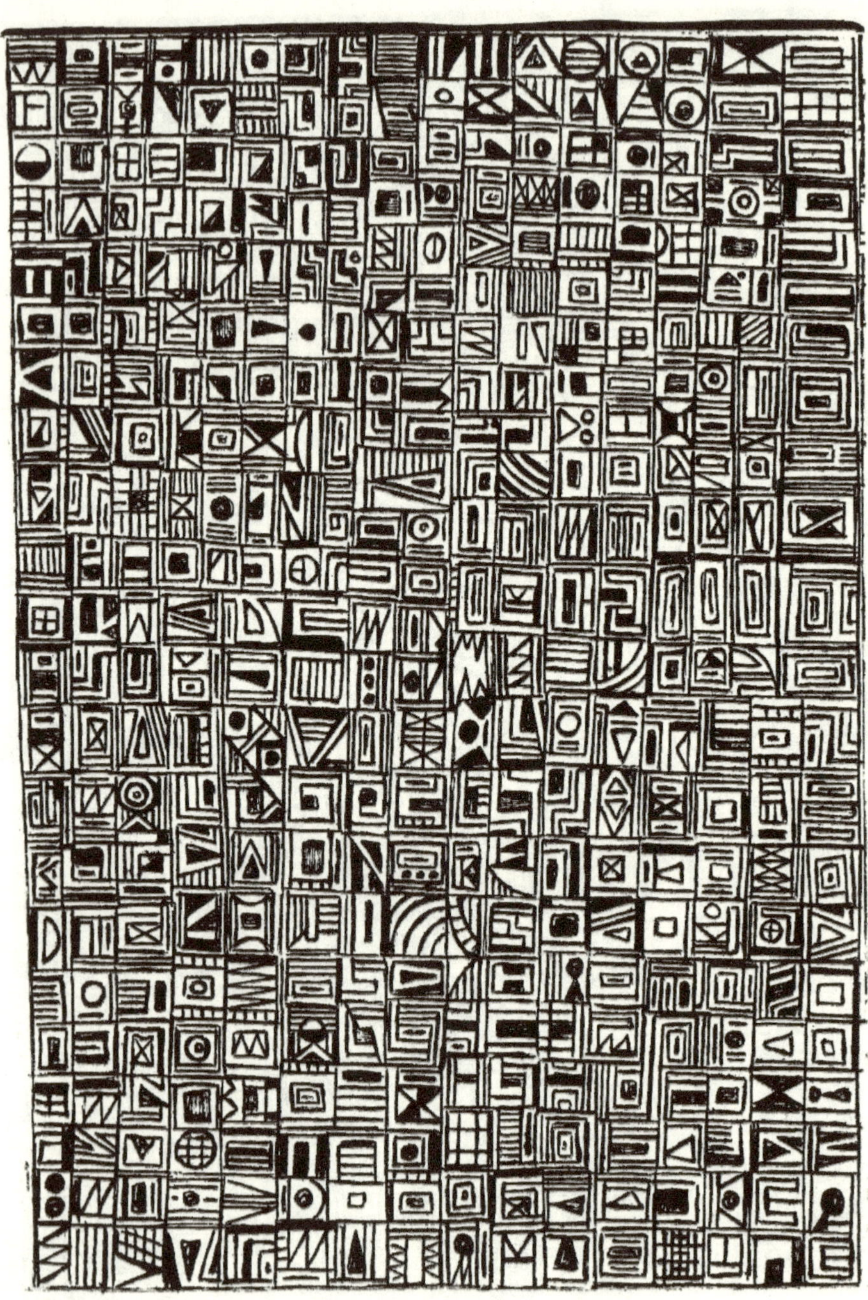

Part 2

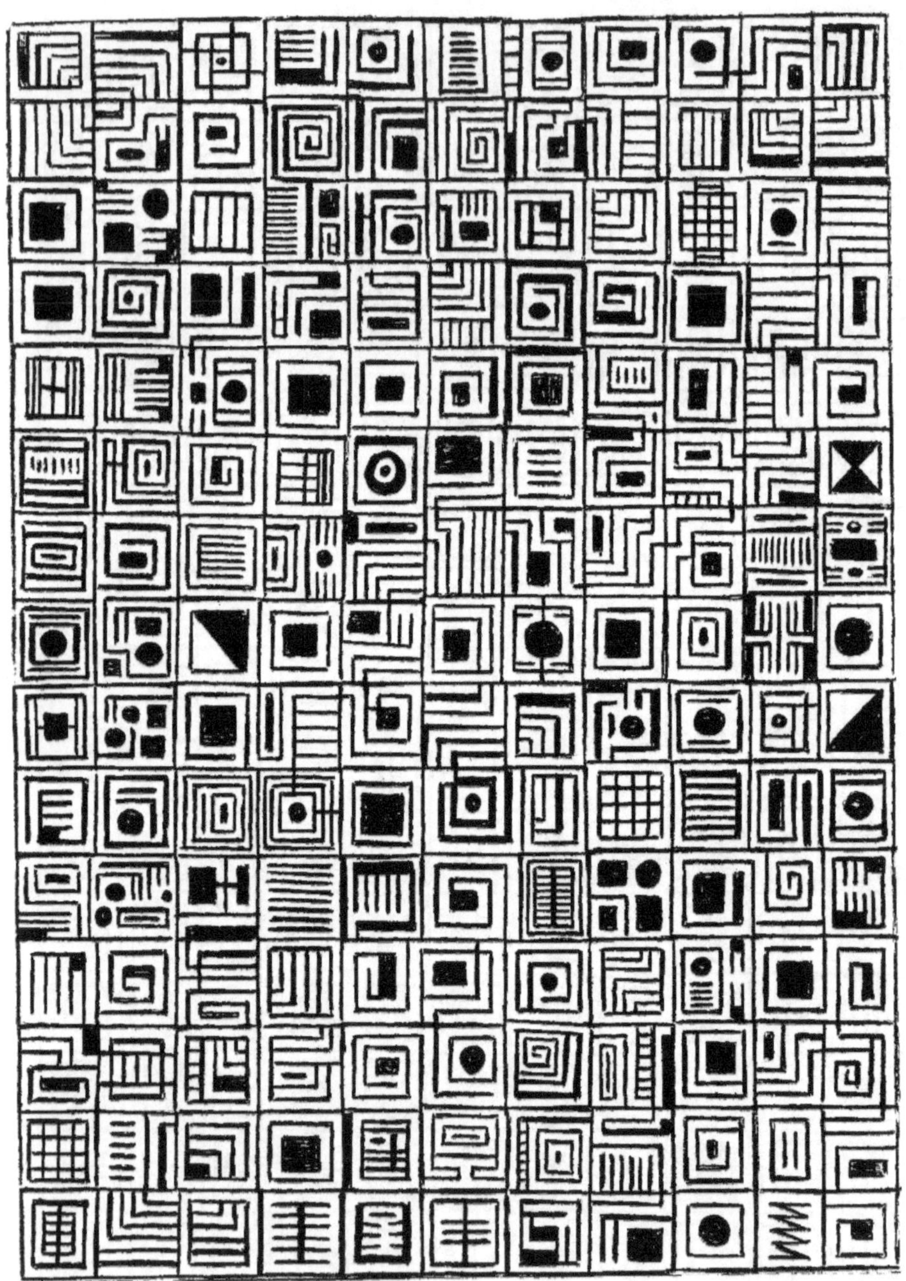

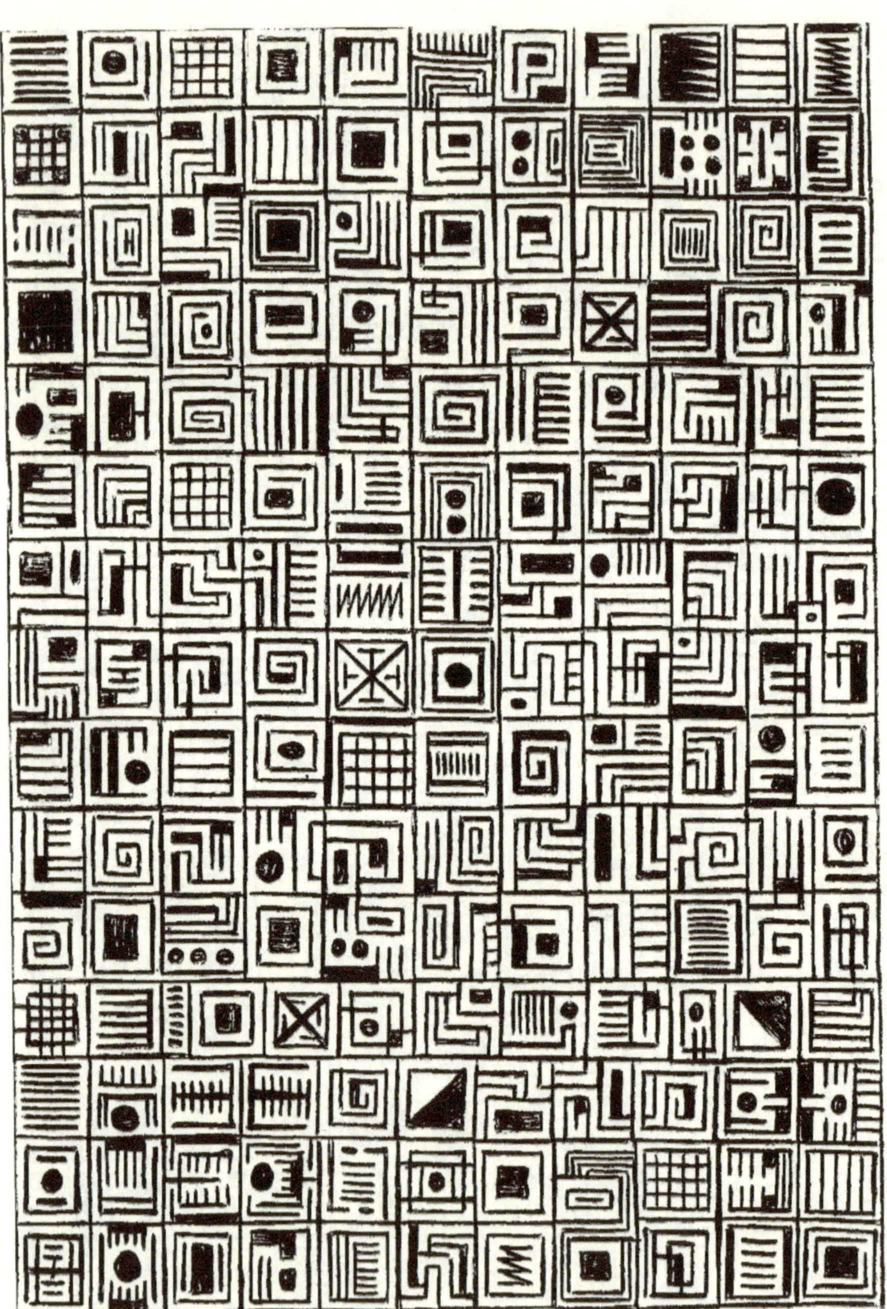

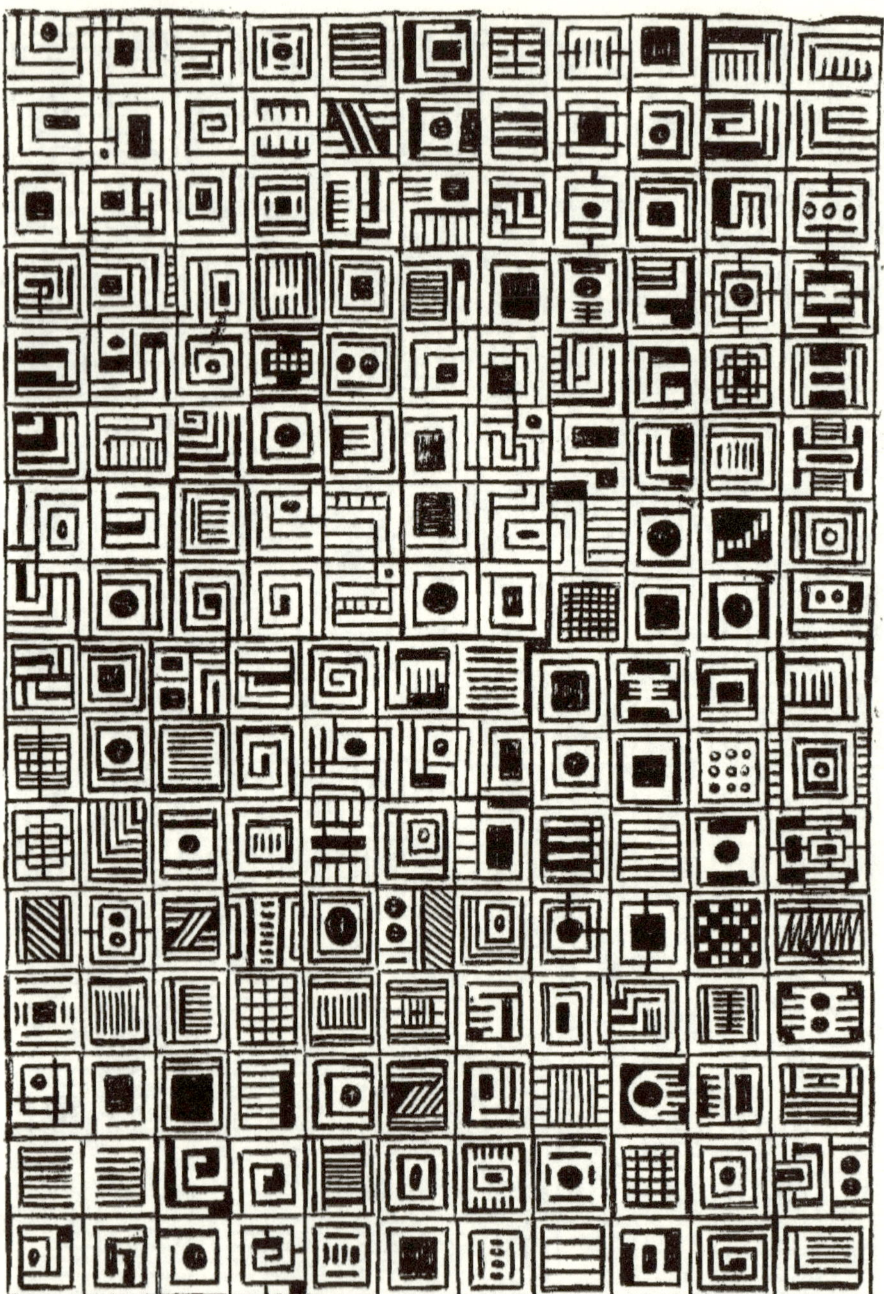

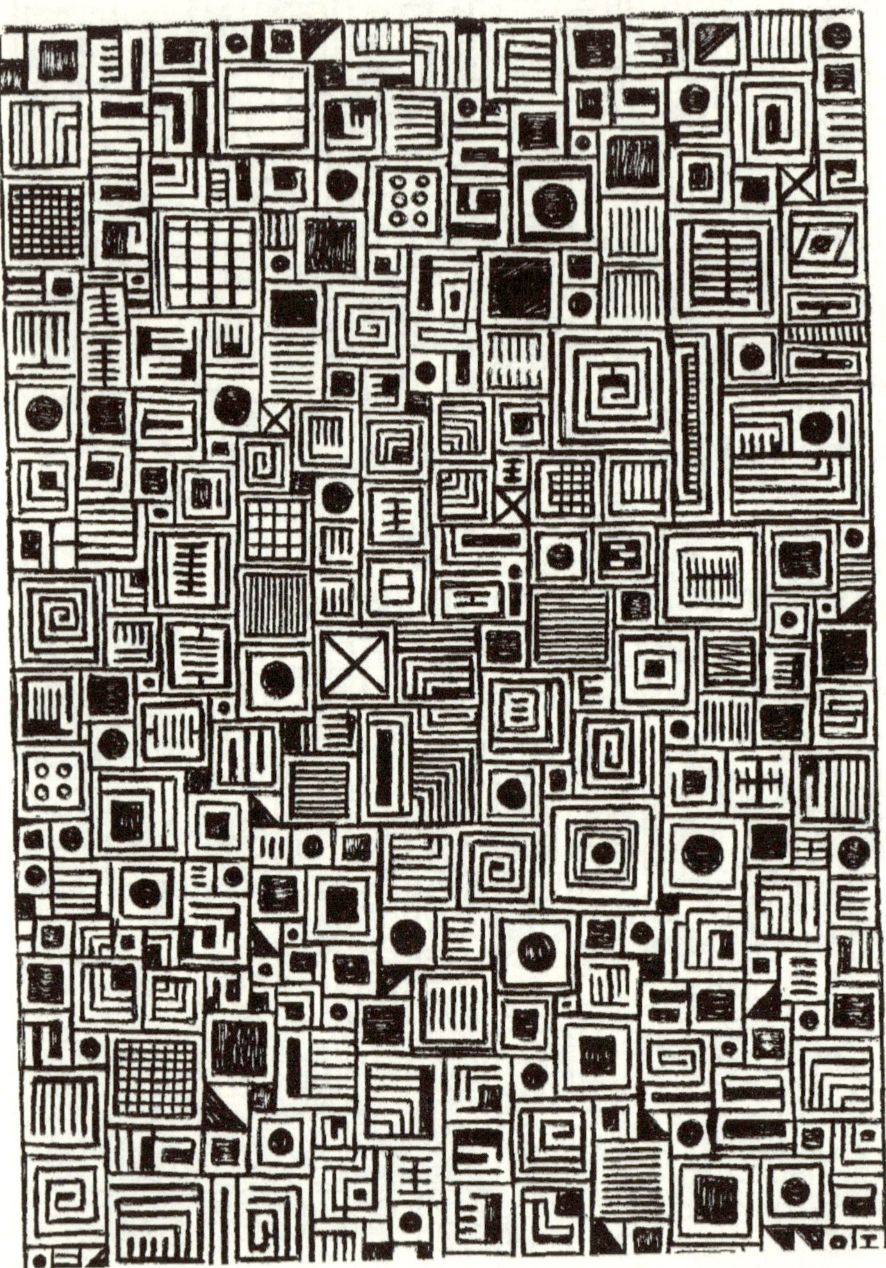

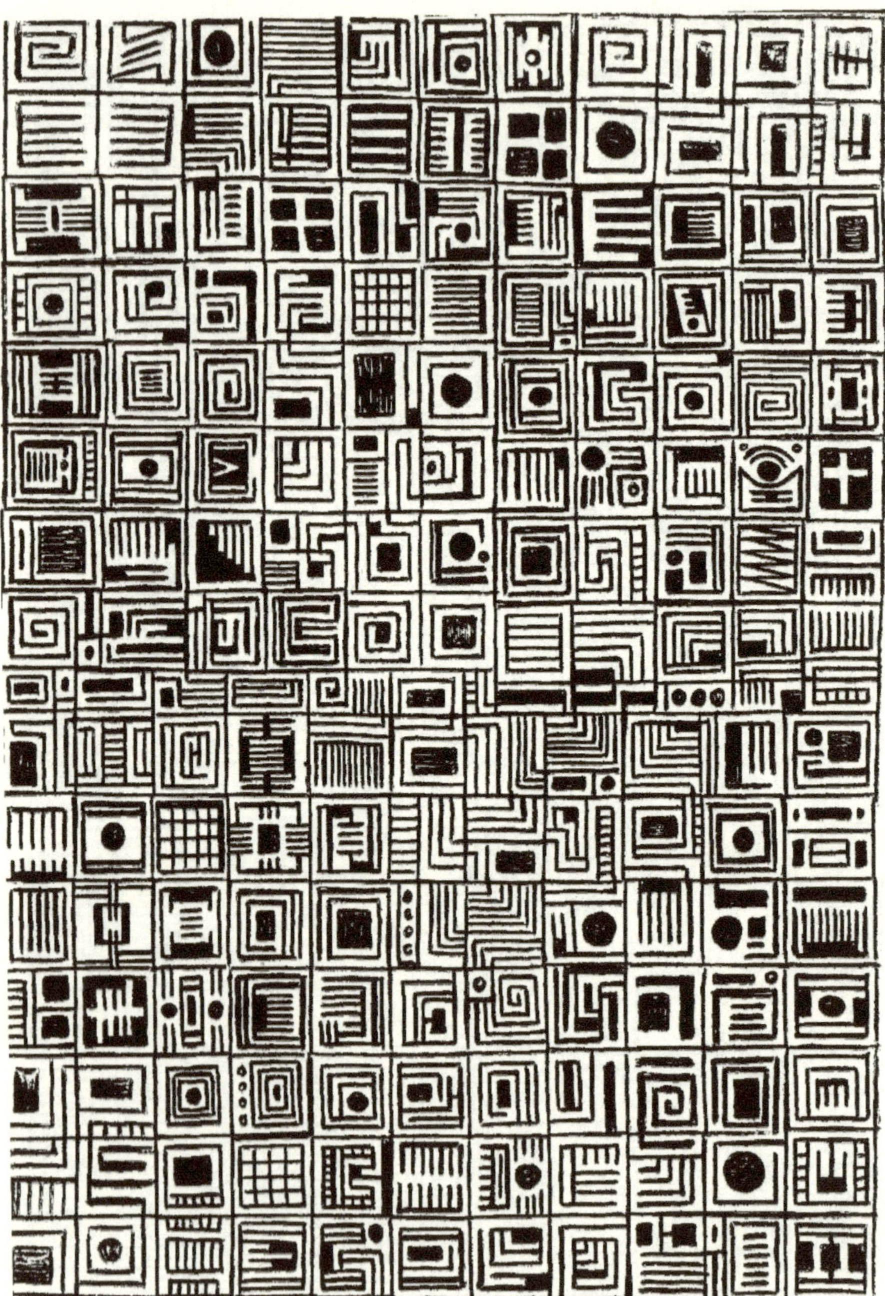

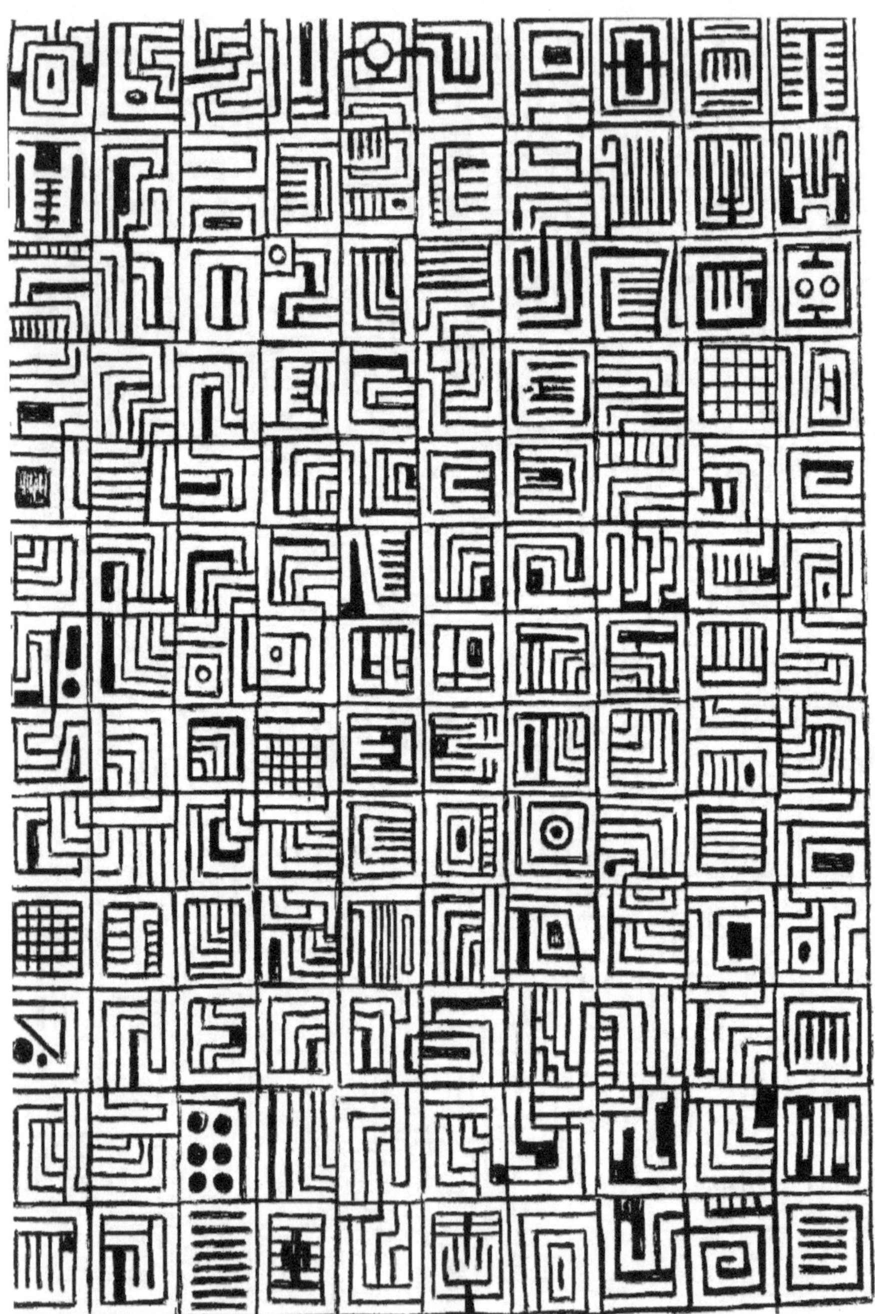

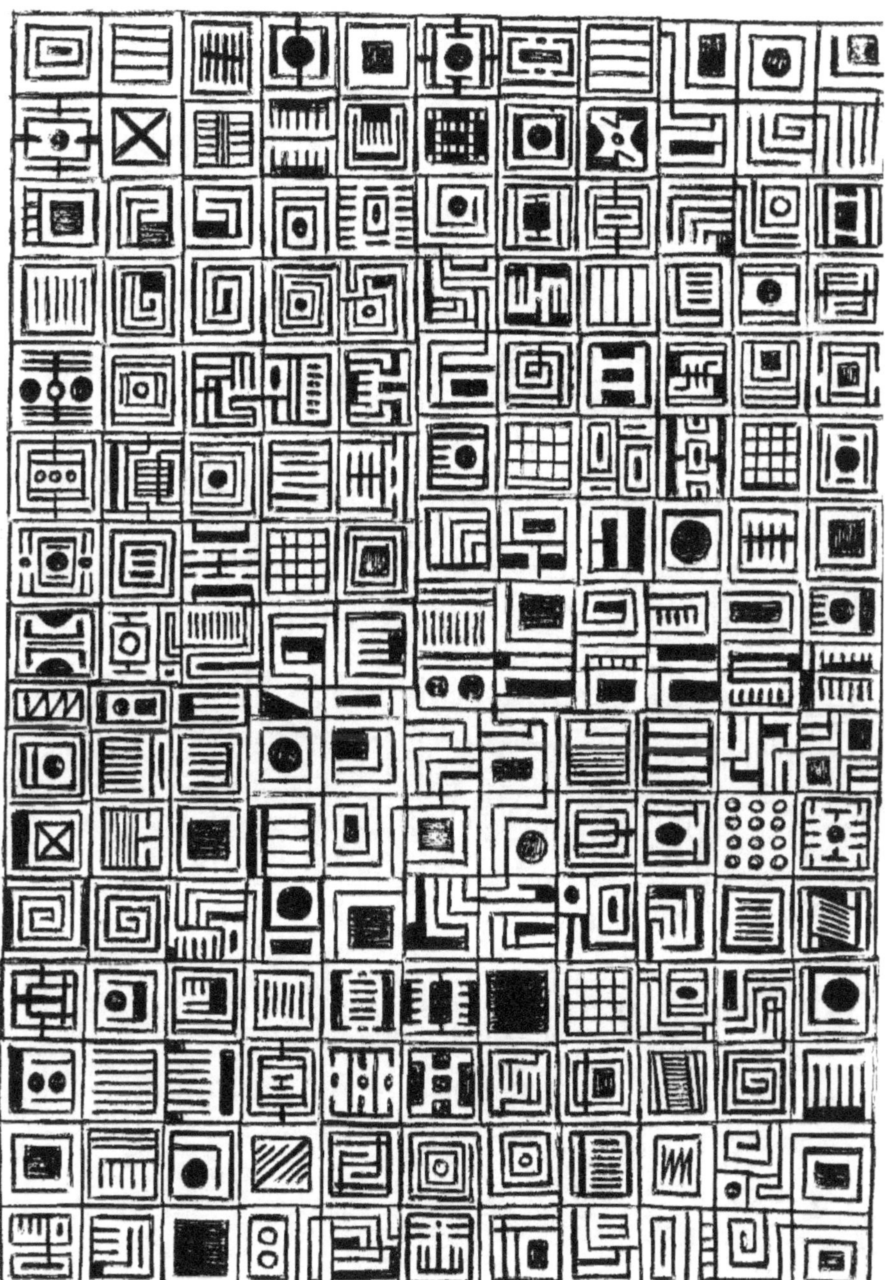

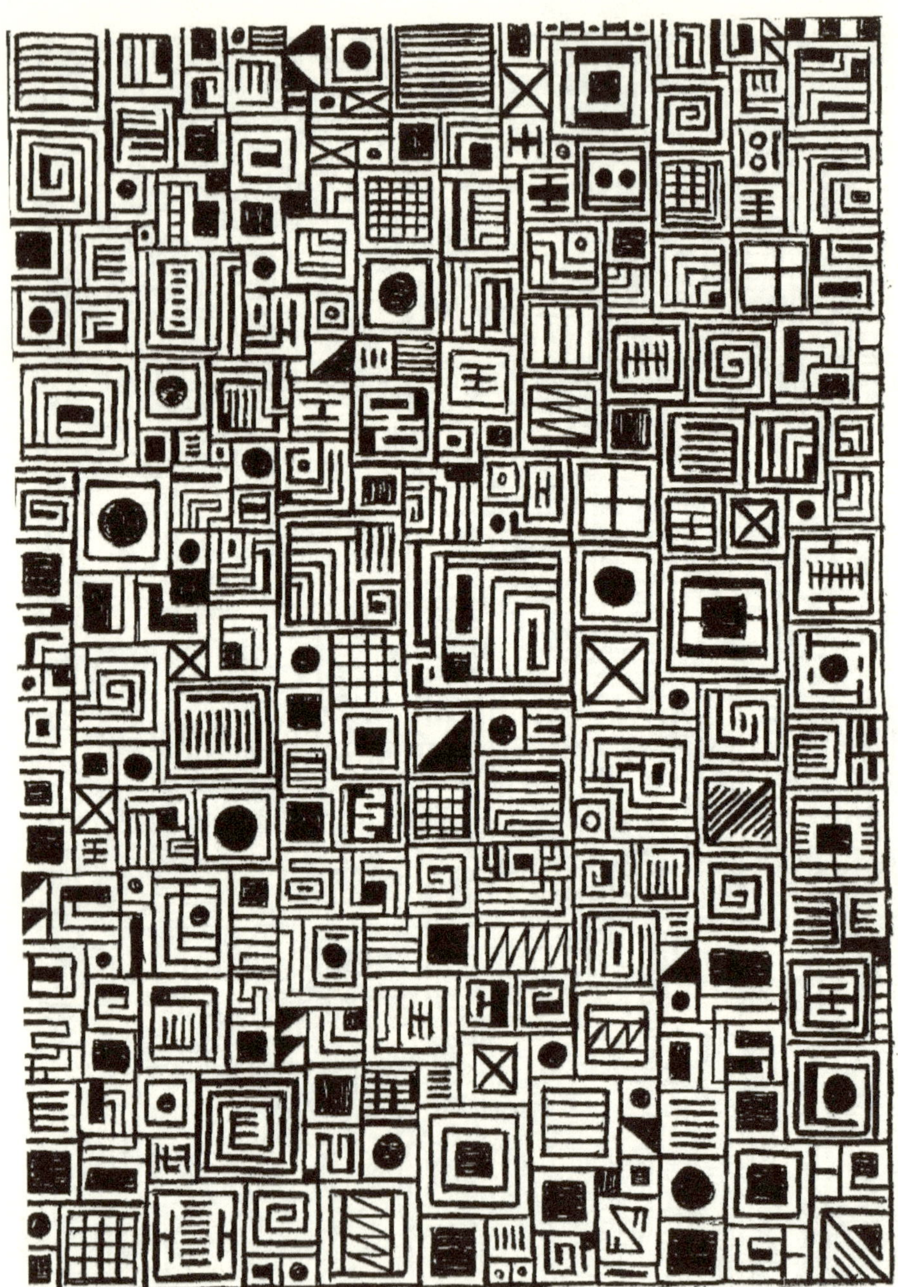

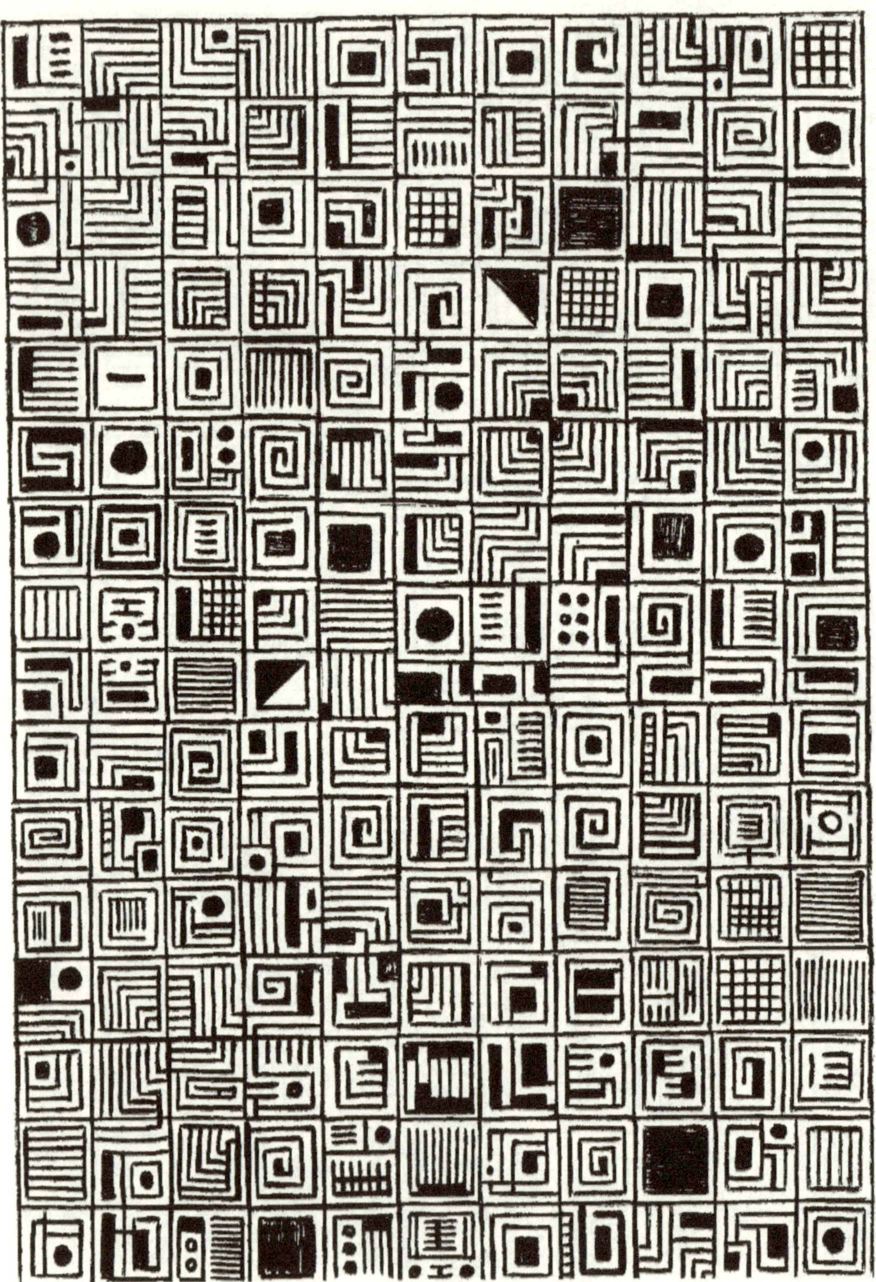

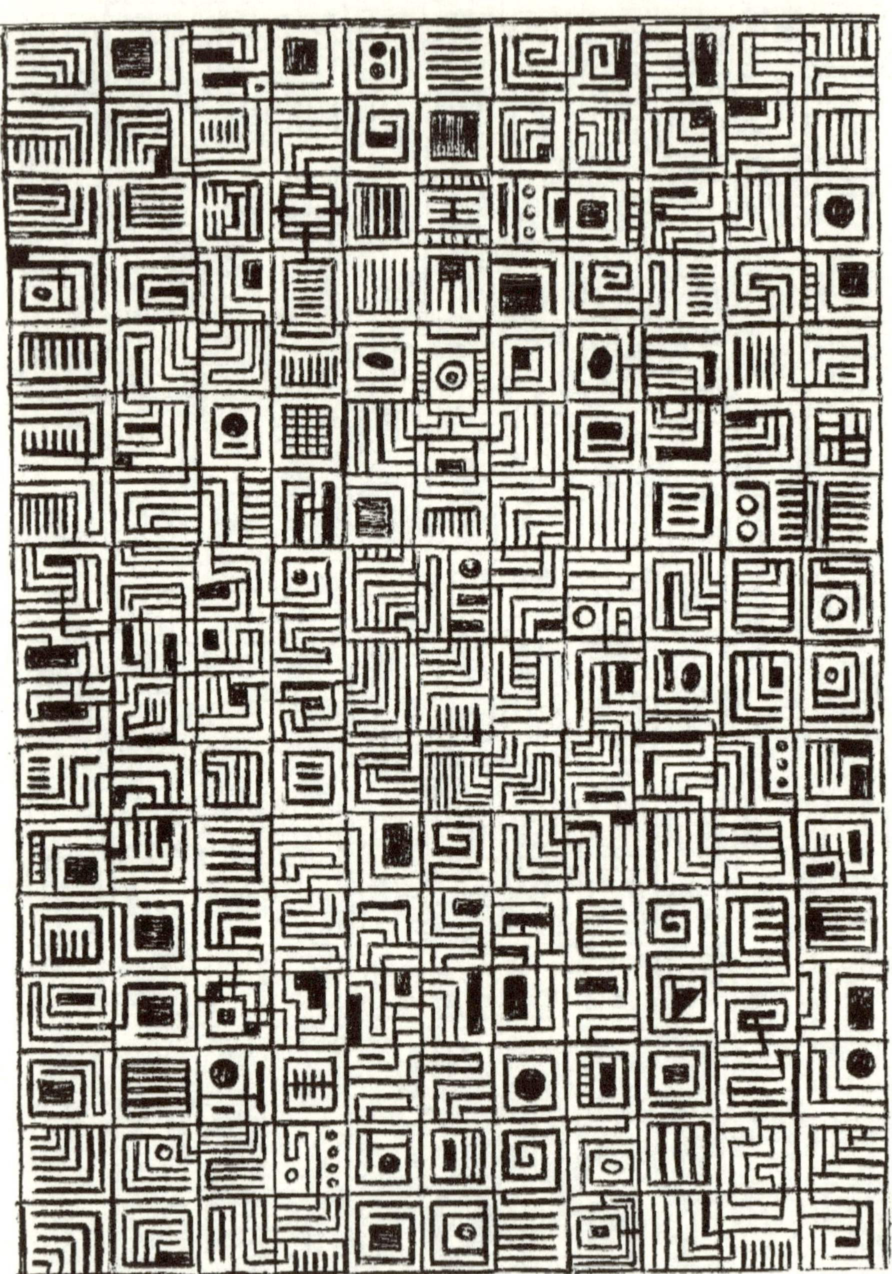

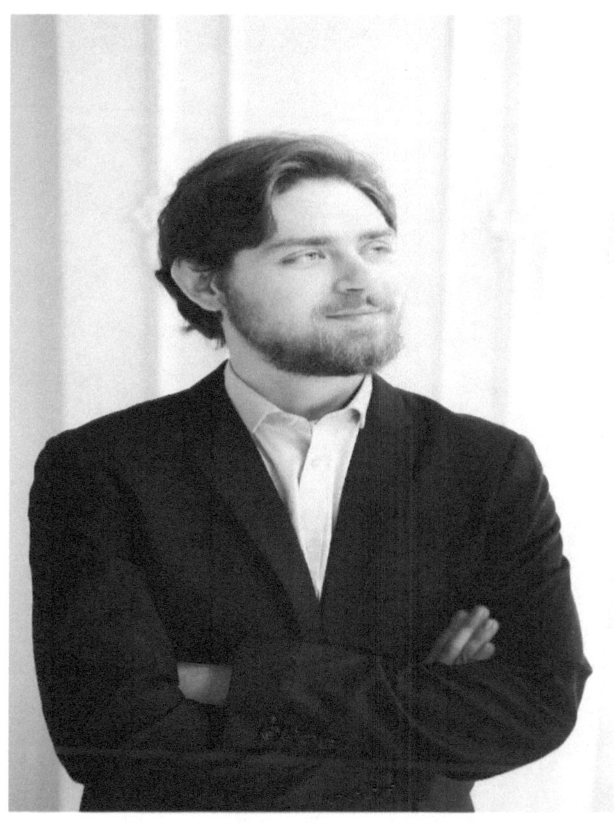

Volodymyr Bilyk is a poet from Ukraine who writes in English. Basically, he's from another dimension or Parts Unknown. Long story short: he follows Ezra Pound's "Make It New" and considers The Pink Fairies song "Do It" to be a quite adequate description of his artistic intentions.

His latest book ***Roadrage*** was published by Zimzalla in 2018. The other works include ***To When Tea Ties Hence to Wank It Too, Eminent Means of Basil Dado Hem-Welt*** (2015), ***Heartbeat, Footclick, Machine Gun Vocalizes*** (2016), ***Eellogofusciohipoppokunurious*** (2017) and ***Lisa Simpson Poems*** (2018).

www.ingramcontent.com/pod-product-compliance
Lightning Source LLC
LaVergne TN
LVHW091012080826
845145LV00003B/1236

* 9 7 8 1 7 3 2 8 7 8 8 6 0 *